T0046860

EDITOR'S LETTER

Royal secrecy has no place in a democracy

Hundreds of documents on the UK's Royal Family have been consigned to a form of historical purgatory. **JEMIMAH STEINFELD** writes on why this needs to end

CHINA'S FIRST EMPEROR did not like history. In 213 BC Qin Shihuang ordered all histories burned, except official Qin records. Three years later he allegedly buried hundreds of scholars alive for owning forbidden books. According to Sima Qian, a historian writing more than 100 years later, the aim was "to make the common people ignorant and to see to it that no one in the empire used the past to criticise the present".

This desire to control the past is not unique to China, nor to a bygone, imperial age. A cursory glance at the last century reveals a plethora of examples. In 1944 Nazi troops set Warsaw's Central Archives of Modern Records on fire, completely destroying the records it housed; the Stasi, who were known for loving paper and possessing few shredders, hastily tore through thousands of documents in their archive

when the Berlin Wall fell. In Russia, Yury Dmitriyev has languished in prison for years due to his research into Stalin's gulags (Putin is trying to rehabilitate the Soviet leader's name). All the while Russian troops ransack Ukrainian libraries, destroying books that attest to an independent Ukrainian past. The instinct to airbrush history is strong and persistant, especially amongst autocrats.

Sadly this instinct is alive in the UK. Earlier this year, I was put in touch with the historian Andrew Lownie. Over a cup of tea, he told me and my colleague, Martin Bright, about his battle to access archives on the Mountbattens, who were in the British Royal Family's inner circle. Spoiler: Lownie did manage to get hold of the archives, and no historians were executed or imprisoned along the way. But it took Lownie years, cost lots of money, some reputational damage, stress. And while Lownie was successful,

he told us the files he struggled to access were just some of many that are denied the British public for no good reason.

We decided to look into this, in part out of genuine interest and in part to channel the message of one of our founders, Stephen Spender, who said that Index wouldn't be doing a good job if we didn't keep an eye on attacks to free expression that happen on home soil. The results of our investigation are eye-opening. The number, and in some cases absurdity, of historic files on the Royal Family that are unavailable is staggering. Many historians and journalists fail to carry out their work fully as a result. In one instance an entire book was panned because of lack of access.

When we started this investigation Queen Elizabeth II was alive. The UK now has a new king, Charles III, who has also been implicated in our special report. As Charles prepares for his first King's speech at Christmas, and the UK prepares for his coronation next year, it's never felt more important to discuss this culture of censorship. We wrap up the year with a simple request: to end this culture by opening up official archives related to the Royal Family. They should belong to the public. Please join us in our campaign to #EndRoyalSecrecy. ✖

Jemimah Steinfeld is Index editor-in-chief

51(04):1/1|DOI:10.1177/03064220221144866

A commonwealth of issues

Mark Frary introduces our cover artist Eria Nsubuga

ERIA NSUBUGA IS from Uganda, where he says self-censorship amongst artists is high and where galleries censor artists too out of fear of the authorities. His work, which has

been exhibited in London, Shanghai, Paris, Milan and Amsterdam among others, explores metaphors of borders and invented nation-states. Shadow of turning/Elizabeth

on the cover and Commonstealthiness on page 50 focus on the legacies of empire. They pull together images of Queen Elizabeth II and excerpts from a book by the British missionary

Reverend John Roscoe. "I use thread as symbolic connections and entanglements within notions of fictional commonwealths and marginal spaces," said Nsubuga.

CONTENTS

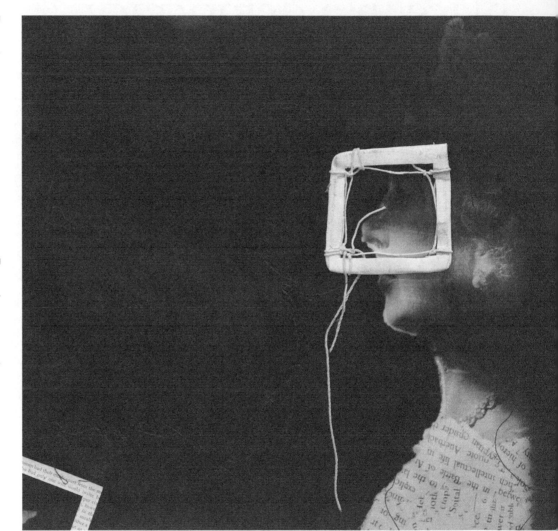

Culture

Comment

The Index

51(04):4/13|DOI:10.1177/03064220221144867

A round-up of events in the world of free expression from Index's unparalleled network of writers and activists

Edited by
MARK FRARY

PICTURED:
Protesters in Port
au Prince, Haiti
burn tyres during
demonstrations against
the government of
Prime Minister Ariel
Henry. In September,
Henry had announced
a fuel price increase
leading to a blockade
of the main fuel port,
crippling fuel shortages
and soaring prices

The Index

ELECTION WATCH

FRANCIS CLARKE looks at what is happening at the poll booths of the world

1. Cuba

MARCH 2023

Elections in Cuba, if you can call them that, for the National Assembly of People's Power will be the first elections since 1976 in which neither Fidel nor Raúl Castro are involved. The elections are run under the one-party socialist system of the country's Communist Party (PCC), so people won't be able to vote for the president or prime minister of Cuba; other political parties are outlawed, independent media is banned and dissent is suppressed. The unicameral National Assembly is directly elected to serve five-year terms, but a PCC-controlled commission designates all candidates, presenting voters with a single candidate for each seat. The president and vice president are chosen to serve up to two five-year terms by the National Assembly, and the prime minister and other members of the Council of Ministers are designated by the National Assembly upon the proposal of Miguel Mario Díaz-Canel Bermúdez who is currently First Secretary of the PCC.

2. Nigeria

FEBRUARY 2023

Nigerian businessman Peter Obi could be an unexpected wildcard for the 2023 Nigerian presidential elections. Drawing comparisons with Emmanuel Macron, Obi is not running on the ticket of either of Nigeria's two main political parties, representing the Labour Party instead. He is seen as a major draw to the nation's younger voters. Over 10 million new voters have registered for the election, most of them youths. The prominent activist Aisha Yesufu, cofounder of the #BringBackOurGirls movement, has endorsed Obi. After reports of misinformation, low voter turnout and intimidation affecting the 2019 presidential elections, Obi is seen as a bright hope for a new generation of voters. President Muhammadu Buhari is stepping down after two terms in office representing the All Progressives Congress Party (APC). Atiku Abubakar of the People's Democratic Party will be the main challenger to the APC's new candidate, Bola Tinubu, who himself has a history of corruption allegations.

3. Estonia

MARCH 2023

Estonia will head to the polls in 2023 after Prime Minister Kaja Kallas of the Reform Party called off cooperation with the Centre Party over a dispute on education. Kallas only became prime minister after the previous holder of the position, Juri Ratas, resigned over corruption allegations regarding an inquiry into a property development. Prosecutors alleged the development was promised permission to build a road on city property, in exchange for a donation of up to one million euro to the Centre Party ahead of municipal elections.

Kallas' centre-right Reform Party emerged as the biggest party in the 2019 elections. However Ratas then blocked the party from taking power by forming a coalition of his left-leaning Centre party, the conservative Fatherland party and far-right EKRE that gave the three parties a majority in parliament.

Estonia was the first country to allow online voting but mobile voting has now been ruled out for the coming election. ✖

BELOW: Miguel Mario Díaz-Canel Bermúdez, first secretary of Cuba's Communist party; Peter Obi (left) and Pat Utomi (right) of Nigeria's Labour Party; Estonian Prime Minister Kaja Kallas

THE LATEST FROM OUR CAMPAIGNS

INDEX ON CENSORSHIP works on a number of active campaigns around the world. Find out more at indexoncensorship.org

Daphne Caruana Galizia: Five years on

It is five years since investigative reporter Daphne Caruana Galizia was brutally assassinated in a car bomb attack in Malta. Index and 35 other human rights and press freedom organisations issued a statement to mark the anniversary and point out the intolerably slow progress of criminal investigations into her murder.

"Impunity serves to embolden those who use violence to silence critical journalism and it ends only when all those responsible for the heinous murder have been prosecuted to the full extent of the law: the assassins, intermediaries and the mastermind must be brought to justice without further delay," the statement read.

The statement continued, "Similarly, we must point out the unacceptable lack of implementation of the recommendations made by the landmark Public Inquiry into Caruana Galizia's assassination and the exclusion of structured public consultation, including with our organisations, on proposed legal amendments relating to the safety of journalists and SLAPPs, which in the latter case fail to meet international standards."

Letter to Foreign Secretary to call for release of Salma al-Shehab

Index continues to act to secure the release of Saudi national Salma al-Shehab, who was a student at the University of Leeds at the time of her alleged 'crimes' – sharing content in support of prisoners of conscience

ABOVE: Investigative journalist Daphne Caruana Galizia was murdered in Malta five years ago; University of Leeds PhD student Salma al-Shehab was jailed for 34 years in Saudi Arabia; Former Kazakh President Nursultan Nazarbayev

and women human rights defenders, such as Loujain Alhathloul. Index has written to the new Foreign Secretary James Cleverly along with a number of partner organisations.

Al-Shehab was sentenced by Saudi Arabia's Specialized Criminal Court, originally set up to try terrorism offences, to 34 years in prison, a sentence four years longer than the maximum sentence suggested by the country's anti-terror laws for activities such as supplying explosives or hijacking an aircraft. Al-Shebad also faces a subsequent 34-year travel ban.

In the letter, Index's policy and advocacy manager Nik Williams wrote, "At a time of significant global uncertainty and unrest, the UK can and must play a leading role in promoting human rights globally. While we appreciate the wide and diverse range of issues facing you and your department, we are contacting you to draw your attention to the treatment of political prisoners in Saudi Arabia who have been imprisoned for expressing themselves."

Anti-SLAPP measures cannot come fast enough

The urgent need to introduce anti-SLAPP measures, proposed by the UK government in July, has been underscored by the recent announcement that a UK-registered company and a Kazakhstan endowment fund have issued legal proceedings against a number of UK media outlets.

Early in 2022, openDemocracy and The Bureau of Investigative Journalism (TBIJ), amongst other outlets, published separate reports on the Nazarbayev Fund and Jusan Technologies Ltd. They have since been threatened with legal action. Index called for the legal action to be dropped and for the UK Government "to be both bold and swift with their proposals to bring forward anti-SLAPP legislation to ensure all public interest reporting is robustly protected against abusive lawsuits". ✖

The Index

PEOPLE WATCH

FRANCIS CLARKE highlights the stories of human rights defenders under attack

Şebnem Korur Fincancı

TURKEY

Şebnem Korur Fincancı is a human rights defender jailed in Turkey as authorities pursue an investigation against her as head of the Turkish Medical Association, which President Reccep Erdogan accused of "spreading terrorist propaganda". Korur Fincancı is also a board member of the Human Rights Foundation of Turkey, and is a retired professor of forensic pathology. Her work was central to the creation of the United Nations' "Istanbul Protocol," a landmark manual on how to identify and document signs of torture.

Fatima Saleh Al-Arwali

YEMEN

Fatima Saleh Al-Arwali, the head of Yemen's Habitat Organization for Human Rights Development, disappeared after posting a tweet in July 2022 that was critical of the de facto Yemeni government. Al-Arwali has ceased all of her activity on social media since her disappearance and there have been conflicting reports of who arrested her, with the Houthi group in the city of Al-Bayda, and the Emirati authorities after she travelled to the United Arab Emirates, mentioned. The Gulf Centre for Human Rights has made an appeal for news of her or her whereabouts.

Elchin Sadykov

AZERBAIJAN

On 10 September, Elchin Sadykov was arrested in Baku, the capital of Azerbaijan, and his home and office raided by the police. Sadykov is a well-known human rights lawyer who has represented politicians, activists and journalists over the years. Issues of freedom of expression, including media freedom, have been long standing concerns in Azerbaijan, and colleagues have said he has been the target of continuous intimidation and harassment for his human rights work. He had reportedly been on hunger strike before his court trial.

Narges Mohammadi

IRAN

Narges Mohammadi was arrested in November 2021 for attending a memorial for a victim of anti-government protester killings in Iran. She has been in confinement since, and was given her third sentence in a row in October 2022 for supporting the right of people to demonstrate. Mohammadi is a journalist and spokesperson for the the country's Defenders of Human Rights Centre and has campaigned for the abolition of the death penalty in Iran. She is facing yet another court case for "civil disobedience" brought against her by intelligence agencies.

Ink spot

Iranian climber Elnaz Rekabi competed in the 2022 IFSC Climbing Asian Championships in Seoul, South Korea in October 2022, where she finished fourth. Her participation at the event proved controversial as she competed without a headscarf, which has been the focus of protests in Iran since the death of Mahsa Amini in the custody of the country's notorious morality police. On returning to Tehran, Rekabi apologised and said her headscarf had accidentally slipped off. Credible sources report that Rekabi was forced to make the apology and has been under house arrest since her return.

Rekabi's plight was highlighted by the dissident Chinese artist Badiucao who has penned this issue's cartoon. He has also highlighted the death of 16-year-old Nika Shakarami, who vanished on 20 September during protests in Tehran and was missing for a week before her lifeless body was found.

869 NEW EXTREMISTS IN BELARUS. IS THERE ANYTHING TO WORRY ABOUT?

INNA KAVALIONAK of prisoner database Politzek.me says Belarus is dangerous, but not because Lukashenka is slapping labels on his opponents

ON 4 NOVEMBER the Belarusian Ministry of Internal Affairs added 244 people to its extremist list. A week before, 625 people were added in one day. It now includes 1,714 people.

Belarus must be so dangerous with this many extremists, right?

New detentions happen every week.

In early November, Darya Losik, the wife of Radio Free Europe journalist Ihar Losik, who had dared to be vocal about the torture her husband had experienced in a penal colony, was herself detained.

From the first day of Ihar's detention, Daria had spoken out about the mistreatment he faced. After he tried to cut his wrists, she recorded a video (**tinyurl.com/Index514Daria1**) appealing to Lukashenka himself.

At Politzek, we ran a big interview with Daria last summer (**tinyurl.com/Index514Daria2**). She seems fearless, but I'm sure she was scared making the appeal. Despite the threats, constant worries about her husband and being forced to raise their three-year-old daughter alone, she's been doing it anyway.

Daria revealed how her daily routine has changed dramatically since her husband's imprisonment. Such stories of everyday heroism are becoming normalised and this is my fear. Such acts should be appreciated and respected.

The official reason for Daria's detention was her interview with the independent media channel Belsat, also labelled extremist.

The state is trying to stigmatise political prisoners further by labelling them in this way.

We are often asked 'Are they real extremists?' The only thing Ihar did was being a journalist; Daria, defending her loved one.

We cannot prevent the lengthening of the extremist list. But being vocal about it in order to maintain their spirit and help their families is possible.

That's what Politzek does. ✖

 We cannot prevent the lengthening of the extremist list

Free speech in numbers

10–18

Years faced in prison by 10 Nubians in Saudi Arabia for organising a symposium commemorating the 1973 Arab-Israeli war

70,000

The number of people who joined decentralised social media platform Mastodon the day after Elon Musk's confirmed takeover of Twitter

8

The number of prisoners killed in a fire at Tehran's Evin prison sparked by protests over Mahsa Amini's death

50.9%

Share of vote received by Luiz Inacio Lula da Silva in the second round of voting in Brazil's presidential election

12 million

Number of users claimed by social network Parler, recently acquired by rapper Ye, after it was kicked off its hosting platform in 2021

The Index

WINNERS OF INDEX'S 2022 FREEDOM OF EXPRESSION AWARDS ANNOUNCED

The "bravery and brilliance" of free expression champions from China, Cuba, Russia and Ukraine celebrated

THE WINNERS OF Index on Censorship's 2022 Freedom of Expression awards were announced at a ceremony in London on 27 October hosted by broadcaster, journalist and commentator Ayesha Hazarika.

The awards, now in their 22nd year, celebrate those who risk arrest, assault and imprisonment through their championing of freedom of expression. This year's panel of judges consisted of multi-award-winning artist Alison Jackson, artist and writer Coco Fusco, journalist Ben Preston and Chair of the Index Board of Trustees Sir Trevor Phillips.

The winners were:

The 2022 Trustees Award - Andrey Kurkov

Andrey Kurkov is a writer, journalist and the current president of PEN Ukraine. Born in St Petersburg in 1961, he graduated from the Kyiv Foreign Languages Institute, worked as a journalist and did military service as a prison warder in Odessa. He became a writer, producing screenplays and authoring critically acclaimed and popular novels, including Death and the Penguin. Kurkov is a hugely respected commentator on Ukraine, and his most recently translated novel, Grey Bees,

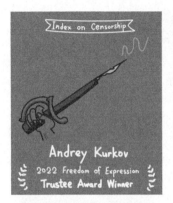

Andrey Kurkov
2022 Freedom of Expression
Trustee Award Winner

OVD-Info
2022 Freedom of Expression
Campaigning Award Winner

Huang Xueqin
2022 Freedom of Expression
Journalism Award Winner

Hamlet Lavastida
2022 Freedom of Expression
Arts Award Winner

explores the current conflict through adventures of a beekeeper. Read an interview with him on p.92.

The 2022 Freedom of Expression Award for Journalism - Sophia Huang Xueqin

Huang Xueqin is an activist and journalist who has reported extensively on the MeToo movement in China. Huang has worked to promote women's rights, and to document and expose sexual harassment against women and girls. She has faced legal challenges because of her work and was detained between October 2019 and January 2020 after writing about mass protests in Hong Kong.

On 19 September 2021, Huang disappeared. It has since been confirmed that she had been detained and charged with "inciting subversion of state power". She remains in detention and is now held in the No. 1 Detention Centre in Guangzhou, southern China.

The 2022 Freedom of Expression Award for Arts - Hamlet Lavastida

Hamlet Lavastida has been described as a political activist by way of art, using his art to document human rights abuses in Cuba and to criticise Cuban authorities. Lavastida has been involved in various protest movements in Cuba, including the 27N movement which grew out of the protests held on 27 November 2020.

In June 2021, Lavastida was arrested after returning from a residency at the Künstlerhaus Bethanien in Berlin. Following his arrest, Amnesty International named him as a 'prisoner of conscience'. Lavastida stayed in prison for 87 days. Lavastida has been living in exile in Europe since September 2021, warned that he will be arrested immediately should he ever return to Cuba.

The 2022 Freedom of Expression Award for Campaigning - OVD-Info

OVD-Info is an independent human rights media project documenting political persecution in Russia. They collect information about detentions at public rallies and other cases of political pressure, publish news and coordinate legal assistance to assist detainees. The organisation was set up in 2011 to document arrests during the widespread anti-fraud protests. The organisation has now evolved to offer legal guidance and support to people arrested at peaceful protests in Russia.

In September 2021, OVD-Info was labelled as a 'foreign agent' by Russian authorities. During the ongoing war in Ukraine and associated anti-war protests in Russia, OVD-Info's work is more important than ever.

Despite a highly unpredictable situation and persistent, or rather increasing, censorship, OVD-Info continues to support detained and persecuted protesters in Russia.

Ruth Smeeth, Index on Censorship CEO said: "Our Freedom of Expression awards celebrate the bravery and brilliance of journalists, artists and campaigners from across the globe. Each and every winner is a beacon for free expression, standing up for their democratic rights and values in the face of often unimaginable personal peril. The quiet heroism of our winners gives us all reason to redouble our work to defend free speech and free expression around the globe, give voice to the persecuted, and stand against repression wherever we find it." ✘

World In Focus: Peru

Attacks on freedom of expression, surveillance and restricted rights to information have become commonplace in the third largest country in South America

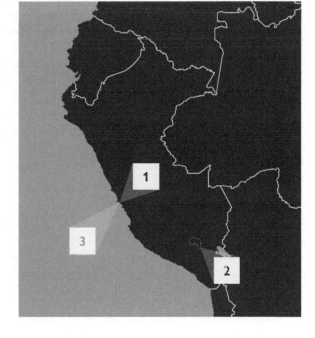

1 Lima

In April 2022, Peruvian President Pedro Castillo threatened to file a criminal defamation lawsuit against two journalists after they reported Castillo's close ties to a man under investigation for corruption.

The threat, in the form of a notarised letter, was made to the editors of the news show Panorama and news website Vigilante. It came after both outlets showed photos of Castillo playing football with a man known as Roberto Aguilar, a public works contractor who secured around $154 million worth of contracts from the Castillo administration.

Castillo denied the man was Aguilar and stated he: "will not allow the abusive exercise of freedom of expression and information… to undermine my authority."

Under Peru's penal code, criminal defamation through the press is punishable by up to three years in prison. To date, there are no reports that Castillo has filed the lawsuit.

2 Espinar

Documents leaked in May 2022 showed the General Directorate of Intelligence of the Ministry of the Interior (Digimin) had compiled information on environmental rights defenders and a journalist during a protest in the town of Espinar in southern Peru, in October 2021. Digimin collected information on at least three environmental defenders, as communities blocked a key transport route in protest at mining activities in the region at the time. Independent journalist Vidal Merma Maccarco was noted in a report as using the cover of an independent social communicator to try and stir up the population of Espinar, allegations which were unfounded.

3 Lima

The Peruvian press has endured a difficult time in the past year during Pedro Castillo's presidency. In April, the Lima-based Institute for Press and Society wrote a letter to the president of congress asking to lift the ban on entry to press areas in congress after pandemic restrictions at a national level were lifted.

Index on Censorship wrote in July about Castillo's silence with the country's press after refusing to speak to it for more than 100 days. As recently as October, it was reported that only foreign media were allowed to attend a presidential press conference, with journalists from Peruvian-based outlets locked out of the room. Reporters were told the government would organise an event for national press later in the day, which did not happen.

The Index

BUYING THE RIGHT TO FREE SPEECH

TECH WATCH

As another billionaire playboy eyes up a tech platform, **MARK FRARY** reports on the hijacking of free expression

IT IS A strange state of affairs when you have to pay, and pay big, to get free speech. In October, it was announced that Ye - the artist formerly known as Kanye West – intends to buy Parler, the self-styled "leading viewpoint-neutral, free speech social media platform". Although the size of the deal has not been revealed, the company has raised

$56 million in investment to date.

Parler launched in 2018. In January 2021, following incursions into the US Capitol building after Donald Trump disputed the outcome of the presidential election, Parler was banned from both Apple's App Store and Google's Play Store for publishing posts that the two app stores said incited violence. It was also kicked off Amazon Web Services, the cloud platform on which it was hosted. In a legal challenge against Amazon's decision, the platform said it had 12 million registered users and claimed that it had a $1 billion valuation. Parler was allowed back on Apple and the Play Store in September 2022.

The announcement of Ye's intention to invest came after he was suspended from Twitter and Instagram for making anti-Semitic posts on the two platforms. The rapper had threatened to go "Defcon3" on Jewish people. Ye later said in an interview with Piers Morgan, "I'm sorry for the people that I hurt

CREDIT: (Musk) Debbi Rowe; (Ye) Parler handout; (Alaa) family handout

ABOVE: Elon Musk has paid $44bn for Twitter and plans to make verified users pay; The rapper Ye is in talks to acquire the self-styled "leading viewpoint-neutral, free speech social media platform" Parler

with the Defcon... the confusion that I caused." However, when asked if he regretted making the comments, he told Morgan: "No, absolutely not."

Free speech is at the heart of Ye's proposed acquisition. Announcing

A very high price

MY INSPIRATION   Campaigner **MONA SEIF** speaks to Index about her brother, the British-Egyptian blogger Alaa Abd el-Fattah

I AM THE middle child of three children and we are less than five years apart. Sanaa is my younger sister. My elder brother is Alaa Abd el-Fattah, arguably the most high-profile pro-democracy activist in Egypt. He has been in prison since the military coup of 2013 for all but a few months.

We grew up very close but Alaa would frustrate me. We are very different personalities. Alaa has always been very outspoken since we were kids. On the other hand, I was really trying to fit in with the crowd and melt away. It was annoying but exciting to have

a brother that rebellious at an early stage.

I actually remember Alaa's first protest; it was in school before Sanaa was born. It was sports day and we were supposed to leave early as it was Alaa's birthday and he had so many plans. Some teacher disagreed and locked all the pupils in the school. Alaa and his classmates were the oldest in the school and started a protest. We ended up being allowed to leave.

Everyone has a special thing they bring to their family. Alaa has a deep connection with everyone

and invests in having shared interests with each and every one of us.

With mama, who is a professor at Cairo University, they would talk for hours about physics and science. With Sanaa, who is a film editor, Alaa would speak about the arts and would point her to a recent thing he had read.

I am a molecular biologist specialising in cancer biology, although I had to give this up last April to support Alaa's campaign. I finished my master's thesis while he was in prison and he read it thoroughly. We had letters back

and forth between us and he would send questions about it. He is the central point of the family, both emotionally and intellectually.

Our nuclear family comes with a long history of political activism. My father was a human rights lawyer. Both he and my mother were politically active. I was born while my father was in prison during Hosni Mubarak's presidency.

Being involved in politics and human rights and being aware of the public sphere was expected of our family. When we rebelled against our parents and tried not being engaged it didn't last long.

the deal, Ye said, "In a world where conservative opinions are considered to be controversial, we have to make sure we have the right to freely express ourselves."

The CEO of Parler's parent company, George Farmer, added, "This deal will change the world, and change the way the world thinks about free speech."

Whatever Ye ends up paying for Parler, he can probably afford it: his net worth has been estimated at somewhere between $2 and $6.6 billion. Parler's price tag is unlikely to be anything like the $44 billion that Elon Musk (world's richest man, net worth $218 billion) paid for Parler's erstwhile rival, Twitter. Musk's on-off deal to buy the platform, which has around 400 million active users, crystallised this October despite Musk's threats to pull out of the acquisition because of arguments over the number of fake users on the platform. Since Musk's acquisition, the company has faced an even more tumultuous period.

Musk's Twitter purchase was also ostensibly about free speech. At the time he said, "Free speech is the bedrock of a functioning democracy, and Twitter is the digital town square where matters vital to the future of humanity are debated."

Ye and Musk are not the only rich and powerful men to want platforms for their free speech. After President Donald Trump was kicked off Twitter following the elections, he announced his company Trump Media & Technology Group (TMTG) would launch its own social media platform, Truth Social, where posts would be called "truths".

At the time Trump said, "I created Truth Social and TMTG to stand up to the tyranny of Big Tech. We live in a world where the Taliban has a huge presence on Twitter, yet your favourite American President has been silenced. This is unacceptable...TMTG was founded with a mission to give a voice to all."

While buying the right to have free speech seems like a modern pastime for rich and powerful men, it is just the channel that has changed. Billionaires have always wanted to buy newspapers and television channels to get their voices heard.

Over the years, Rupert Murdoch has bought the Wall Street Journal and the New York Post, The Times and Sunday Times as well as News of the World and The Sun. In Australia, his company has a stranglehold on media, owning most of the major urban news titles as well as The Australian. Murdoch also owns Fox News and Sky.

Amazon founder Jeff Bezos bought the Washington Post in 2013. That same year, Boston Red Sox and Liverpool F.C. owner John W. Henry bought the Boston Globe.

So Ye's purchase of Parler is hardly groundbreaking. When a rich, black woman buys into the latest free speech platform, now that will be news. ✖

Alaa found his way into politics with the blog Manalaa which he set up with his wife Manal Hassan and which aggregated different Arab bloggers. It was meant to help create an online discourse and help activists self-organise.

He was always quite a force and he was always quite inspiring to my generation which was slightly younger than his. We never foresaw the price he would pay for this with nine years of his life in Abdel Fattah al-Sisi's prisons.

Sisi fears that Alaa and others who are languishing in prison are symbolic of the powerful uprising of 25 January 2011. Sisi and those around him feel their whole existence is challenged by them. We also have a president who takes everything personally. He is a dictator general who shouts and expects people to do what he says. He is bringing the country to its knees just to punish a few youths who said something he does not accept.

Being a family of a political prisoner in the very violent environment of Sisi's Egypt changes you. One of the things I developed over the years is acknowledging the things that are out of my control

ABOVE: Alaa Abd El-Fataah and his sister Mona Seif in happier times; Alaa, Mona and their mother Laila Soueif

and focusing on the things I can influence. I have now acknowledged that the most important thing is not that you remain physically intact but that you sustain your emotional and mental wellbeing

while preserving your self-respect. But you pay a very high price to sustain these things.

Mona Seif is co-organiser of the Free Alaa campaign, **freealaa.net**.

FEATURES

"In an unprecedented move, the Turkish parliament ratified a law in October that means citizens accused of spreading disinformation can be jailed for up to three years."

KAYA GENÇ | THE TRUTH IS IN THE TELLING | P.27

Mexico's truth stares down barrel of a gun

As the secretive Mexican army solidifies more than a decade of control over domestic security, **CHRIS HAVLER-BARRETT** asks what lies in store for a country already marred by generations of violence

PICTURED: President Andres Manuel Lopez Obrador accompanied by Secretary of National Defense Luis Cresencio Sandoval and Secretary of the Navy Jose Rafael Ojeda Duran during a commemoration of the 212th anniversary of Mexico's independence, September 2022

PUBLICLY, THE MEXICAN armed forces are at the head of a brave new humanitarian mission. The nationwide DN-III-E intervention plan has seen the Ministry of Defence (Sedena) take charge of relief operations, infrastructure projects and, as of October, public safety until 2028.

With sweeping new powers, Sedena has absorbed all federal security forces, including the police. The nominally independent navy, Semar, is under the direct control of President Andres Manuel Lopez Obrador and is subordinate to the army.

Lopez Obrador recently won a referendum designed to underscore the support for his continuing term as president, and Mexico is venturing into the wider global community, offering to

> "They have no transparency," he said. "They can basically do whatever the heck they want to do, with impunity."

support peace negotiations in Ukraine, normalise diplomatic relations between Cuba and the USA, and take a decisive stance against transnational migration.

This is all part of the grand Fourth Transformation of Mexico ("4T"), the lynchpin of the legacy project undertaken by Lopez Obrador and his Morena party. The move to deploy the military on the streets is designed to project the success of the 4T into every community in Mexico.

Given this public profile and the political success that Sedena has →

→ seen, it might seem as if the military in Mexico is a beacon of peace and security in a country that is no stranger to savage violence. But this is a long way from the truth.

There is a list of towns whose names stand out from an exhausting roll call of atrocities committed against civilians over the past decade. Apatzingán. Tlatlaya. Ocotlan. Camargo. Ayotzinapa. These towns have all seen violent massacres at the hands of state security forces.

In Apatzingán, the army and federal police opened fire on civilians, killing 16. In Tlatlaya, the army killed 22 people in a massacre that the Washington Office on Latin America (Wola) described as a "complete disregard for human rights and due process". In Camargo, 19 migrants were found mutilated and burned near the US border. Twelve members of the police were arrested for their murders.

But it is the events that took place in Iguala on the night of 26 September 2014 – the Ayotzinapa affair – which are indelibly etched into the public consciousness. The abduction by members of the military, law enforcement and cartels of 43 student protesters travelling to Mexico City, alongside the murders of six witnesses, remains at the forefront of political discourse in the country. Only charred fragments of bodies have ever been found.

The affair was the start of a long and arduous trail of public inquiries, recriminations and, ultimately, a refusal to acknowledge responsibility – turning a national tragedy into a national outrage.

This outrage is fuelled by a military that has blocked scrutiny at every turn. After the arrest of Captain José Crespo in November 2020, Sedena ceased co-operation with the Truth and Access to Justice Commission and has since moved to separate itself entirely from the reach of judicial oversight. During this time, the department of defence, under the command of the mysterious Gen Luis Sandoval, has moved to

consolidate power and cement the office as the primary keeper of law and order within Mexico.

Beyond simply refusing to co-operate, the initial report into Ayotzinapa – labelled the Historical Truth – has proven to be a falsified account of events designed to shift culpability from security forces onto organised gangs operating in the Iguala area. Most of the architects of this report are now in prison or have fled abroad in an attempt to evade prosecution.

Stephanie Brewer, Mexico director at Wola, has been monitoring attempts by Sedena to obscure its role in civilian killings, especially in relation to the events of Ayotzinapa.

"Soldiers essentially saw and knew part of what was happening without intervening to search for or protect the students," she said. "From those early moments, the military did not turn over, or make available, information in its possession for the purposes of searching for the victims [or] for the criminal investigations.

"But what's become known now – largely through the work of the independent expert group (GIEI) and also through the accompaniment of the families of the victims, the NGOs who

By simply paying bribes, cartels are able to operate almost unhindered, moving merchandise, money and weapons freely across Mexico

represent them and now the work of the government-created Truth Commission – is that really, until today, Sedena has still not turned over all the information it has."

Beyond Ayotzinapa, Sedena has been working hard to expand the control and monitoring of media outlets and public bodies to prevent the release of information that may be harmful to their reputations. Journalist Pablo Morrugares, who claimed to have conclusive evidence of military involvement in Ayotzinapa, was found murdered. Although it is not known who was behind the murder and Morrugares of course worked in a dangerous area, his death has still raised suspicions.

A number of investigators and witnesses have also fled Mexico seeking protection from the US government. The identities of potential informants in legal proceedings are often leaked, which has led to the belief that the leaks are specifically designed to help Sedena identify potential threats.

Perhaps worse than the massacres and extrajudicial killings which appear to be committed by the military are the cartel connections. While in a country as deeply penetrated by corruption as Mexico it is to be expected that cartels have infiltrated the army, the true extent of the penetration into national security is shocking.

Gary J Hale, the former chief of intelligence at the US Drug Enforcement Administration, and later Baker Institute fellow for drug policy, has monitored the relationships between cartels and the Mexican state since the 1970s. Across two terms in Mexico, he has personally witnessed the extent of the corruption that undermines the effectiveness of the military. "99.99% of their corrupt involvement never sees the light of day. They do a good job of staying under the radar," he said.

"Within our US government, federal law enforcement and intelligence capabilities, we routinely saw military

ABOVE: Artworks in Mexico City in 2014 display the faces of two of the 43 students from Ayotzinapa school, in the state of Guerrero, who went missing

officers at the flag rank – that's the general level – corrupted. Particularly in the army.

"The Mexican military has been notorious for being corrupt... There is some internal system within Sedena where they almost compete for some of these positions, because wherever it's a hot zone... then that's more opportunity for making money through bribes.

"This corrupt arrangement [is] always done at the general level, because the general has control over everybody in the chain of command below him."

The military works hard to obscure the true extent of the corruption plaguing them. The arrest of a former senior military official for working with cartels was quickly swept under the rug, and the official was not prosecuted, despite being apprehended by US authorities.

This last case perfectly encapsulates the issues surrounding the Mexican military. It encapsulates the lengths to which Sedena will go in order to obscure their involvement with organised crime.

Despite ample evidence that the official had been, at best, laundering money for – and, at worst, a member of – the Beltran-Leyva cartel, the government dropped the investigation against them as soon as the DEA released the former minister to Mexican authorities.

The efforts of the military to suppress freedom of speech go much further than simply falsifying reports and dropping investigations. Researchers tasked with uncovering the events of Ayoztinapa have reported heavy surveillance.

The military has also been accused of compiling dossiers on lawmakers and government bodies, according to emails recently obtained by El Pais as part of the massive Guacamaya hack of Sedena email servers. It is unclear what Sedena was using these profiles for.

In the most extreme cases, the dossiers contained the blood types, school histories and personal information of politicians and appear to have been designed to help the military identify key political players in every region of Mexico, as well as potential

threats to their control. Politicians who requested information regarding the Ayotzinapa affair appear to have been singled out.

Compounding the constitutional and human rights issues faced by the new laws, oversight of Sedena and military operations is largely non-existent.

The new security laws mean that the military, who are unable to be tried by civilian judges, will instead be tasked with self-policing, using only military tribunals to determine whether they are guilty of wrongdoing.

Hale is direct in his assessment of the existing tribunals: "If they have investigated and punished their own people, they sure the heck haven't told anybody. So, the assumption is they have not."

As a result of the unwillingness to prosecute offenders, Hale feels that the legitimacy of Sedena has been compromised. "They have no transparency," he said. "They can basically do whatever the heck they want to do, with impunity."

The recent Guacamaya hack vindicated many of those who claimed that the military had been operating unchecked for too long. Direct evidence of military commanders supplying weapons to cartel members has come to light – troubling news for those who hoped the government would stand up to the criminal organisations that effectively function as the de facto rulers of many areas of the country.

With the military neutralised at the highest level by simply paying bribes, cartels are able to operate almost unhindered, moving merchandise, money and weapons freely across Mexico. This is particularly evident in hotly contested regions of Mexico and especially in the state of Guerrero, where Ayala is located.

How has a government body that appears to be so willing to commit extrajudicial killings and defy accountability risen to such a position, especially under a government that   →

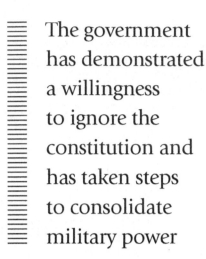

The government has demonstrated a willingness to ignore the constitution and has taken steps to consolidate military power

→ considers itself to be representative of Indigenous and minority Mexicans? The answer is twofold.

First, the government of Lopez Obrador is a government that finds itself in need of public reassurance. The public policy of *abrazos no balazos* (hugs not bullets) has simply led to a situation where the cartels have become more brazen, organised and heavily militarised.

Second, the politicisation of the office of commander-in-chief – held by the minister of defence – has allowed Morena to install party loyalists at the top of the pyramid, both in Sedena and in the covert intelligence community.

While the reforms which passed the Senate in October officially allow the military to take control of on-the-ground policing and security throughout Mexico, this is little more than a formality after more than a decade of military activity. Brewer is direct in assessing the seriousness of this situation.

"This last reform, making the National Guard part of the Armed Forces, that is of course a red alert," she said. "That's a step backwards but it's really kind of the last nail in the coffin. It's a step backwards following many years of growing militarisation, especially in these last few years of the Lopez Obrador presidency."

Roberto Lopez Barroso is a human rights activist and international lawyer based in Mexico City. He has been following the increasingly frantic attempts by Morena to demonstrate that they control the national security situation in the lead-up to the 2024 presidential election.

"According to the constitution, public security is a state-only responsibility. Two laws have been drafted to try to elude this statement," he explained. "The [most] important one is Ley De Seguridad Nacional, which uses dubious and [inexact] vocabulary to try to make the difference between national security and public security blurry and inexact."

These powers are, nominally at least, new and radical. In passing the law, the government has demonstrated a willingness to ignore the constitution and has taken steps to consolidate military power directly under the control of Sedena. Lopez Barroso notes that the steps taken by the government to implement the deployment are in direct contrast to Mexican political and legal tradition.

Brewer agrees that the decision to take federal policing – the only nationwide form of law enforcement in Mexico – under the wing of Sedena marks an attempt to exert increased control of the general population, and describes it as "alarming". Today, with the absorption of the federal police, it is difficult to leave the house without encountering an officer who is under Sedena control. Military patrols are not an uncommon sight on the roads, even in the capital.

Critics claim that Lopez Obrador has increasingly been discussing his desire to remain in his post for a second term – something explicitly forbidden by the constitution.

The ban on re-election, a holdover from the revolution which ousted dictator Porfirio Diaz after seven terms, is seen as paramount to the integrity of a system already struggling with severe corruption. Several media outlets have become concerned by these actions – an alarm compounded by recent statements by Obrador, who on 24 October suggested that "we could consider proposing a reform to increase the term of the presidency".

The future of Mexico under this officialised intervention looks uncertain. While military policy is nominally non-interventionalist, the reality for many Mexicans is one of tight control.

Brewer is uncertain that the militarisation will be reversed in the near future.

"In practice, it's already hard once you give something to [the] military … to take it away, and by giving all this to the military instead of investing in civilian institutions, you're cancelling, or at least hampering, those institutions' ability to evolve and to become strengthened."

Hale is more pessimistic in his assessment of the future, suggesting that the actions of Lopez Obrador constitute "a coup d'etat in the making".

"Typically, when a junta occurs under this concept, the military makes a soft coup d'etat and … the military takes over and they're going to run the country, and they do everything. They are now the secretary of defence, the secretary of agriculture, the secretary of education, the secretary of transportation," he warned.

"How they get there is not important. It could be that it was a coup d'etat and that caused the junta to occur, or it could be like what's happening with Amlo [as the president is widely known] and that's what I'm warning about. It's slowly consolidating all power, and by this, I'm talking about military power, into one entity, with one chief. Who is the commander- in- chief? [Lopez Obrador]."

Exactly what Obrador intends to do with his newfound control – and whether it is even the elected government which is really in control – remains to be seen. ✖

Chris Havler-Barrett is a journalist based in Mexico

51(04):16/20|DOI:10.1177/03064220221144878

The war the world forgot

A new book, an excerpt of which is below, shines light on the scale and depth of Yemen's ongoing civil war. **JEMIMAH STEINFELD** spoke to the book's translator, **SAWAD HUSSAIN**, about getting the story out

A FEW YEARS AGO, the civil war in Yemen made regular headlines. Not so today, despite the fact that the conflict is far from resolved.

"Yemen has been forgotten," said Sawad Hussain, the translator of a new book about the war by journalist and writer Bushra al-Maqtari. What Have You Left Behind is a vignette of interviews with people across Yemen. Hussain was already familiar with the author – she'd translated some of her fiction and been, in her words, really moved by it. So when she discovered al-Maqtari had non-fiction work based on her journalism, it sang to her.

"It's very rare to come across non-fiction translated from Arabic to begin with, let alone non-fiction that is chronicling a war that is ongoing... When I read it I was just really convicted that this had to [be translated] into English," Hussain told Index.

Hussain, who majored in Middle Eastern studies, added: "If someone like me, who keeps up to date with everything, has also forgotten about it then how much more is the average person going to know what is happening in Yemen? And that's why I said yes."

Translating it was far from straightforward. There were the logistics. Al-Maqtari lives in Sana'a, the capital of Yemen, and was reachable only via email – at least to begin with. Collecting the stories that make up the book (which were recorded over two years from 2015) was dangerous and risky work, and Hussain, who often has a very close relationship with the writers she translates, had to play by different rules. Communication was kept to a minimum, in part to not open up past traumas unnecessarily and in part to protect al-Maqtari.

"I was always distinctly aware that I should be careful of what I was saying, and I would always preface it with 'As you said in the book', just making sure that this is not some conversation about what she is planning, because she is an activist," said Hussain.

Another challenge was the material itself. The pain of those interviewed is breathtaking. It stays with the reader long after the book is put down.

"The process of translating the book was extremely traumatic," said Hussain. "I had never worked with something this visceral before in terms of the descriptions of the dead and just the raw emotion of loss and the fact that I kept thinking 'These are real people'.

"Each time I'm seeing the names of these people, I'm seeing the ages, I'm seeing the number of children they've lost."

Hussain was a new mother at the time of starting the translation. It was in the middle of the Covid-19 pandemic and she was far from her family. Reading about the young children who were killed left her "kind of paralysed". She described having nightmares and then feeling torn.

"I'm only translating this. I'm not living this," she said. This conflict, in turn, made her more determined for the book to reach a wider audience, for the voices of those featured within its pages to be heard in English.

Still, she couldn't escape the extreme anxiety that working with this material day and night created. She was more apprehensive than at any time in her life. And this from someone who is no

ABOVE: Yemeni writer and journalist Bushra al-Maqtari, pictured in 2021

stranger to conflict.

"I grew up in Karachi [in Pakistan]. I have grown up around guns, I have grown up around violence. I know people who have been in hostage situations, people who have been held up – that's normal for me. But this was a different kind of violence, an everyday violence that doesn't stop."

In order to cope with translating the material, Hussain attended a workshop on translating traumatic literature where she connected with other people working on equally difficult projects. She found it helpful to hear about their strategies for coping. She made sure to meet friends, to take breaks and, as a faithful person, to pray.

As for al-Maqtari, she remains in Yemen today (with a string of awards now to her name). Whether for emotional reasons or out of safety, she is currently not doing interviews.

"I'm in awe of her making the decision to stay," said Hussain.

"She's been offered asylum and she's refused because for her, I think, it's really important to stay with the Yemeni people in her country where things are happening... It hasn't abated, it's not any easier than it was before." And that remains the point – to remind people that tragedies continue in Yemen, even if no one reports them.

Jemimah Steinfeld is editor at Index →

Extract from What Have You Left Behind?

by Bushra al-Maqtari

THIS IS THE APOCALYPSE, NOT WAR

At the al-Dehi checkpoint,[1] the soldiers' faces change just as their filthy uniforms do, but their weapons remain aimed at our heads. Their aggressive tone may change, the weather may change, but we women of this city never do. We, who are under siege, with nothing left at home to eat. We have to repeatedly risk crossing this death strip. There are women as far as the eye can see, some of them in lines, others in circles. Sometimes they stand in the street or sit on the pavement facing the crossing, protecting themselves from the sun with cardboard boxes over their heads. Next to them are empty gas cylinders and their young children.

At various times and places, I remember leaning on my cane, walking long distances on my exhausted feet, fear in my heart. But hunger forces me to take the risk. If the soldier was preoccupied, sometimes just by coincidence I could cross over to the market on the other side of the checkpoint. I'd buy what I needed and return safely home. Other times the soldier would forbid me to pass, and I'd stand next to the gate, my anger choking me.

One day during the blockade, the gas ran out at home once again. My daughters were worried, and forbade me from going to al-Dehi, but I went out behind their backs. Exhausted, I reached the crossing and tried to walk through, but the soldier blocked me. I swallowed my anger and stood to the side. Dozens of women were waiting, like me, to be let through. Looking at the crowds of women made my blood boil. Another day, I crossed the al-Dehi checkpoint and bought a sack of potatoes. By chance that day a friendly young man said, 'Khala, I've got two gas cylinders here, but I'm sure the soldier won't let me bring them in. How about I push the shopping trolley for you and you add my cylinders to your sack?' I agreed, but when we reached the gate, the soldier blocked me, pulled a dagger from his belt and slit the potato sack open.[2] The potatoes rolled everywhere.

I remember a sad day at al-Dehi, when one of my daughters had insisted on accompanying me. The road to the checkpoint was full of women. I stood with the women, waiting for the soldier to let us pass. First the soldier shot into the air, and then he aimed his gun at the women's feet to stop them going any further. My daughter was among those women. As the women screamed, the taste of humiliation shot up from my stomach to my mouth. 'Why are you shooting at us? Do we look armed?' I protested. He barked, 'Taiz women are animals.' I then said, 'Taiz women will fight you where you stand, and twenty others like you.' He then yelled, 'What do you want old woman?' 'I want to buy food for my children.' 'Go on then,' he said. 'But I need my daughters, I'm sick and I can't carry everything.' I called out some names and many women ran towards me. The soldier blocked them. 'They're all your daughters?' I said, 'Shame on you, let them pass to buy their children food.'

We were risking our lives standing where we were, and if we backed down or turned away, they'd never let us cross again. On the way back, we faced another soldier; an even ruder, heartless man. He didn't respect my old age and screamed in my face, 'Go back old woman, you won't get through here.' 'Will you keep us at yours then?' I asked. There was a man from the Habashi Mountain area, a Houthi sympathizer, who said, 'Khala, don't play with fire, you'll get burned.' I responded, 'He can't touch me.' We walked a little further towards the gate. My daughter was afraid we'd get shot. I really was taking risks that day, the life-or-death kind of ones. At that time the price of a gas cylinder had reached 9000 riyals. We barely made it out. [She laughs.]

Another day, I went to al-Dehi, and their leader himself was there. They were calling him by his code name, Abu Ali;[3] a scary-looking man. I'll never forget his face. I heard later that a woman at the checkpoint had poisoned him. I also heard another story where he was found murdered. What we went through at the al-Dehi checkpoint, I can't put into words. One time, the militia arrested a young man who was just trying to buy food for his family. They beat him up and humiliated him in front of the women. Another man, an ice cream seller, was also beaten by a soldier in front of us, but the man didn't scream or cry out even once. He just kept staring into the soldier's eyes. My heart broke for this poor young man, and I told the soldier, 'Shame on you boy, why are you kicking him like this? He's human, just like you.' He growled, 'Move it before I stick this in your stomach.' He had his hand on his dagger.

One woman was with her son, who couldn't have been more than sixteen years old. He couldn't bear the way the soldier humiliated us women. When he cursed the soldier, he was dragged away to a shop. The militia had turned the shops at the al-Dehi crossing into prison cells, keeping young men locked up in there and torturing them. His mother threw herself to the ground, sobbing, kissing the soldier's boots. 'I beg you, he's all I have, take me instead, and let him go!' Another elderly woman argued with the soldier; he kicked her really hard and pushed her, and she rolled off the main road, crashing into a tree.

I can't even describe the humiliation we endured at that checkpoint; the soldiers' curses, their abuse. One day, I was walking with great difficulty, leaning heavily on my cane. A soldier joked, 'No trouble walking to Sanaa! Sluts.'[4] I answered him, 'We walked because we are brave.' Fear was always in al-Dehi, even after we passed the gate. We'd make our way to the souk, scared. We never used our phones, never picked up our family's calls. We'd walk with our heads lowered, afraid of the snipers hiding atop the buildings.

After the resistance liberated the al-Dehi area,[5] the bodies of soldiers and militia resistance fighters remained on the ground for days until they started to rot and stray dogs began to eat them. I didn't go to see their corpses. My daughter went with the rest of the spectators; she recognized the body of the soldier that had cursed and shot at us.

Whenever I pass by al-Dehi today, I avert my eyes so that I don't remember all we went through there. I've never seen anything like it, my girl. I'm now sixty years old; I've lived through the many wars that have come to this country, but none of

them were like this. Back then, the fighters had morals at least, some sort of humanity. They didn't attack women, torture prisoners, or kill children. When the revolution broke out in the city of Taiz on 26 September 1962, my husband was one of the first to fight against Imam Ahmad. When he was wounded in battle, he went on to join the National Guard in Sanaa, and fought there as well. But neither side committed massacres like this. All the terrors we have lived through in this war I can't even describe. This is the apocalypse, not war.

Khadija Mohammed Hassan

Khadija Mohammed Hassan played a significant role in breaking the blockade the Houthi-Saleh militia imposed on the city of Taiz, after a military checkpoint was erected in the area of al-Dehi. Khadija risked her life helping numerous others enter al-Dehi, and shared with them what she could bring from the souk. She talked of the blockade days with bitterness, about what the women there had faced, how they had been humiliated and degraded. I visited her at her home in Wadi al-Madam in Taiz. By candlelight she talked of the blockade days and the war, or the apocalypse, as she calls it.

*Translated by **Sawad Hussain***

*What Have You Left Behind? by **Bushra al-Maqtari** was published by Fitzcarraldo Editions in October in the UK and will be published in February 2023 in the USA. The excerpt here is printed with their permission.*

[1] *In July 2015, Houthi-Saleh militia set up a military checkpoint in the al-Dehi area, west of the city of Taiz, and enforced a fatal blockade on the city's families.*
[2] *At the al-Dehi checkpoint, Houthi-Saleh militia wouldn't allow citizens to buy more than a kilo of vegetables.*
[3] *Houthi militia always give their fighters code names to conceal their identity*
[4] *The soldier was referring to the Taiz women's participation in the 'March for Life' (20–26 December 2011) from Taiz to Sanaa, a distance of 256 kilometres. The march took place as a protest against the regime of Ali Abdullah Salih. Bushra al-Maqtari was herself one of the leaders of this protest march.*
[5] *The resistance liberated the al-Dehi crossing in March 2016*

51(04):21/23|DOI:10.1177/03064220221144879

LEFT: 1968 Soviet invasion of Czechoslovakia

A dissident hero

Index on Censorship was born out of resistance to Soviet repression. **JO-ANN MORT** met the dissident **PAVEL LITVINOV** to talk about his role in the founding of the magazine, Russian imperialism and the war in Ukraine

PAVEL LITVINOV, WHO recently turned 82, is an imposing figure.

When I meet him on a rainy August day, he fills the space in his compact living room in the suburban New York City garden apartment he shares with his wife, Julia Santiago.

We picked the day, 22 August, for our interview out of convenience, but it happens to resonate. It was on 21 August 1968 that Soviet troops invaded Czechoslovakia, demolishing the "socialism with a human face" of its leader, Alexander Dubček.

Days later, at noon on 25 August, the then 28-year-old physicist Litvinov, with seven comrades – including the group's organiser, poet Natalya Gorbanevskaya (and her baby in a pram) – met in Moscow's Red Square to unfurl a banner that turned out to be life-changing.

Its message was plain: "Hands off the CSSR [Czechoslovak Socialist Republic]." Within minutes, the KGB arrived to forcibly take them away to camps or psychiatric hospitals.

Litvinov, hit hard in the face, was arrested and sent to internal exile in a Siberian mining town for five years with his then wife. His daughter was born there.

"I was in prison for several months and then in exile and had to work in the mines. I couldn't leave the village; I couldn't get permission to travel," Litvinov said. Recalling his motivation for the action, he added: "It felt internally necessary. I had a very strong feeling of what is fair and unfair, and that people have to treat each other gently and with respect."

The Litvinov family was well known in both dissident and Soviet ruling circles. His grandfather was Maxim Litvinov, once Joseph Stalin's people's commissar for foreign affairs until he was deposed in 1939 because, as a Jew, he became an obstacle to warmer ties with Adolf Hitler.

"I was 11 when my grandfather died; we were good friends," he explained. "He was already disappointed in the Russian revolution and the Bolsheviks."

His parents' home was a gathering place for dissidents. Literature also inspired him.

"Most important was Russian literature from the 19th century – Pushkin, Tolstoy, Lermontov... They expressed a feeling of compassion toward helping others under the autocratic state," he said.

Indeed, books and literature, in the form of *samizdat*, were crucial – not only the literary classics but also records of the dissidents' trials in real time.

Litvinov deconstructs the *samizdat* publication process for me, explaining how, during these trials, somebody would gain access to the court and bring the information home.

"They would write the transcript by hand; then we would find someone who had a typewriter," he said. "I would print pages on very thick photographic paper. The book would be photographed and developed in a dark room. Sometimes we would have a party to read the book. I would read the first page, give [someone else] the second page, who would give it to the next one. We would read Doctor Zhivago in half a night, then have tea or vodka. Then I would give a film to a friend from Leningrad, and someone would come from Kyiv – same procedure."

From his earliest dissident days, Litvinov's strategy was to appeal to allies outside the Soviet Union. And that's the connection to Index on Censorship.

In 1968, he co-wrote with dissident Larisa Bogoraz an Appeal to World Public Opinion, about dissident trials.

"I wrote the appeal in Russian. Some of the foreign correspondents translated it to English. In the evening we would always listen to the BBC. They started to speak about the letter. They said Stephen Spender read about it… and Spender called Igor Stravinsky, Mary McCarthy [and] famous American and English writers and composers. They started to interview them. It was so touching when they interviewed Stravinsky. He was 90. He said – in Russian – 'My teacher [Nikolai] Rimsky-Korsakov suffered from Russian censorship and that's why I signed this letter, because these people protested against censorship'."

The appeal didn't keep Litvinov and his group out of prison, but it did have global political impact, opening a path between Litvinov and Spender. And it led to the creation of Index on Censorship.

"Mary McCarthy said that the letter had more influence than napalm did in Vietnam," he said proudly. "Our fight was a fight for freedom of speech, a protest against censorship. Censorship could be when they don't let you publish a book, or when you lose a job, or when you get kicked out of the country, or when you get put in prison. All that means censorship."

Just before the Red Square demonstration, Litvinov sent a letter to Spender suggesting an international council to support democracy in the Soviet Union, along with a publication to promote the situation there.

"When I returned [from Siberia], there was a young man – now I realise that he was 10 years older than I, but he looked younger. He said: 'I am Michael Scammell. I am a Russian specialist'."

Scammell asked Litvinov if he knew more about what Scammell was doing now. "I said 'No'," he recalled, with a smile appearing after all these decades.

Scammell said: "You gave me my first job. I was a writer and journalist. Now I have a job at a magazine as editor of Index on Censorship."

The idea that Litvinov had broached with Spender had come to fruition in his absence thanks to him, Stuart Hampshire, Scammell and others.

"We became friends and Scammell was eventually kicked out of Russia," Litvinov remembered.

Scammell organised lectures for Litvinov at British universities and invited him to join the Index editorial board, which he did for a while.

I wonder whether Litvinov thought that repression could return to Russia after all this time. Indeed, today, he sees a direct line to what's happening there.

"It is a continuation of the kind of thing that happened with Russia and Czechoslovakia. Ukraine was [always] a threat to the Soviet empire. It was clear for all of us that if Ukraine would survive on its own there would be no more Soviet Union. So, there was always tension. In the Stalinist labour camps, half of the political prisoners in the Gulag after World War I were Ukrainian… people strongly felt their national identity and culture. A lot of dissidents became our friends."

But he didn't consider war. "I really didn't expect it until the last minute. Russia really has to lose badly or Russia will start another imperialist adventure," he said.

I wonder, too, about his assessment of Vladimir Putin. He is quick to respond. "In the 1930s, there were very terrible KGB people but among them there were at least people who were ideological communists. In Putin's generation,

they didn't believe in communism or Marxism. They believed in secret police and dirty tricks and spying."

He describes his surprise at how so many people find Putin palatable.

"I always thought that because he was KGB, he was bad. He said he was proud of the KGB. The KGB executed millions of people and he is still proud. If he would say they did some good things and some bad things… but nothing."

In 2006 he retired from his 30-year job as a science teacher at a Westchester school and today he stays in close touch with those who have left, and continue to leave, Russia. He does what he can to support dissent inside the country, especially backing a new generation with fundraising and encouragement.

"There is a group to whom I am very close – OVD-Info. The guy who started it is in Germany and they are available 24/7. If someone is arrested anywhere in Russia, they can call them and, in an hour, there will be a lawyer at the police station. They are the next generation of dissidents."

Does Litvinov have any regrets, having performed heroic actions that exiled him from his birth country?

"This was the whole fun of it," he said. "I enjoyed my life. I was not afraid. I was ready for much worse conditions than I had in Siberia. Then I emigrated and saw America and Europe. I feel like I am more American than Russian."

Before leaving, I ask him if he has hope. He sighs and at first responds: "Oh, hope."

I think he will say "No", but instead he says: "Now, with the war, strangely enough there is more hope. Because it looked like Putin had a good chance, he had so much control, but now because of the crazy war that makes no sense, he probably won't survive for long. What will happen I don't know. [But] I think the war will kick him out. If the war is over, practically Russia cannot win." ✖

CREDIT: Hum Images/Alamy

Mary McCarthy said that letter had more influence than napalm did in Vietnam

Jo-Ann Mort is a US-based journalist

51(04):24/25|DOI:10.1177/03064220221144880

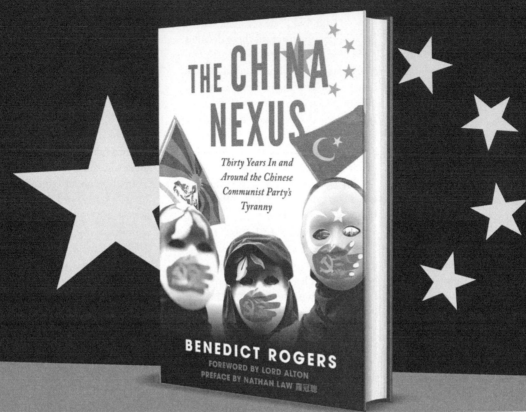

The truth is in the telling

The Turkish government has waged a convenient war on 'misinformation' ahead of the general elections next year. **KAYA GENÇ** looks at how truth has been weaponised in Turkey over the decades

RECEP TAYYIP ERDOGAN'S "New Turkey" never ceases to amaze. Its latest invention is a "ministry of truth" in all but name. Founded in August under the auspices of Turkey's Communications Directorate, the Centre for Combating Disinformation will be "a powerful tool in our struggle for truth," according to an official press release. Since October, the centre has been issuing weekly Disinformation Bulletins, the function of which became apparent the same month, days after a mining disaster in the northern province of Bartın claimed the lives of 42 miners. That week's bulletin picked on journalists who pointed to reports issued by the Turkish Court of Accounts between 2017 and 2019, warning against the security risks of the coal mine whose owner is a close ally of Turkey's ruling AK Party.

"It's wrong to claim that the warnings and recommendations of the Turkish Court of Accounts were not taken into consideration by the coal

ABOVE: A person outside a coal mine after an explosion in Amasra, Turkey. Reporting on the disaster led to accusations of disinformation

> They began releasing 'lies of the week' reports to pick on critical reporters in a concerted effort to get their journalism banned

mine," the Disinformation Bulletin read. "In fact, the firm followed these recommendations and took even more precautions than necessary."

These "truths" – favourable for a government ally and officiated by government officials – were not merely instructive. In an unprecedented move, the Turkish parliament ratified a law in October that means citizens accused of spreading disinformation can be jailed for up to three years. According to the Law To Combat Disinformation, those found guilty of intentionally publishing news which the government claims endangers the overall health of society, or spreads panic, can be sentenced.

A coalition of 22 international press freedom organisations accused the bill of providing "a framework for extensive censorship of online information and the criminalisation of journalism, which will enable the government to further subdue and control public debate in the lead-up to Turkey's general elections in 2023".

Considered alongside the Centre for Combating Disinformation and its Disinformation Bulletins, these developments constitute a warning to anyone willing to dispute the official truths of Turkey's Islamists. Whatever they say goes; those daring to question their truths should prepare for prison.

The prospect of a government-issued truth regime began in 2013. As environmentalists, feminists and other progressive groups filled Gezi Park in Istanbul, the coverage of Turkey as a model Middle Eastern democracy began to crumble in Western media outlets and the speeches of Western politicians. To fight such "prejudices of the West", the Turkish government began its assault on outlets such as The New York Times, The Guardian and →

ABOVE: A Disinformation Law protest organised by the Izmir Journalists Association, held on 21 June 2022. Its President, Dilek Gappi, believes the law could destroy media freedom in the country

→ others. Journalists and intelligence operatives associated with the Turkish government appropriated the term "fact-checking". They began releasing "lies of the week" reports to pick on critical reporters in a concerted effort to get their journalism banned. In numerous cases, reporters lost their jobs; some were imprisoned; a few had to flee the country for safety.

Burcu Karakaş, a reporter for the Milliyet newspaper, was among the first wave of victims of pro-government "fact-checking" campaigns.

"In 2015, a troll site targeted me twice for my reporting and announced that I was a terrorist," she told Index. "Their posts reached not only me and my colleagues but also my bosses, the people at the top. Of course, they knew I wasn't a terrorist, but the headline asked, 'How can Milliyet employ a terrorist?' and that did the job." After Karakaş was fired, the website celebrated the event.

Koray Kaplıca, the director and co-founder of Doğruluk Payı, a genuine Turkish fact-checking initiative, says that the period between 2013 and 2015 was crucial in building the current regime.

"The Gezi protests of 2013 was our beginning point," Kaplıca told Index. "People saw the biases of the traditional media when they refused to cover Gezi protests in the heart of Istanbul."

As students of Turkish political history, Kaplıca's team first studied Turkish disinformation in the early 20th century. The anti-Christian pogroms of 1955 (up to 37 people are thought to have died during the attacks, 1,000 were injured and around 300 Greek women and boys were raped) began with fake news about Greeks bombing the home where Mustafa Kemal Ataturk, the founder of modern Turkey, was born in Thessaloniki.

Another horrific event, a massacre in Kahramanmaraş in December 1978, started with news of a bomb thrown into a cinema attended by nationalists. Left-wingers were rumoured to have thrown the bomb, and the resultant massacre against Alevi Kurds – perpetrated by the far-right organisation The Grey Wolves – killed 175 and injured 3,000.

"Disinformation and misinformation were part of propaganda wars between the right and the left in the 1960s and 1970s," said Kaplıca. He explained that the hatred of different political and ethnic groups lay in the DNA of numerous Turkish political movements.

"Anti-Americanism has been prevalent among conservatives, as well as anti-Semitism," he explained.

"This resulted in the production of disinformation and polarisation. When you look at party programmes of

Turkish nationalist and Islamist parties of the early 20th century, there are so many instances of disinformation against Jewish people and the USA that we can say the general content of Turkish political culture is based on misinformation and conspiracy theories. They're Turkey's default mode."

When Doğruluk Payı launched with a crew of three people in June 2014, two months before the presidential elections, its first task was to fact-check political speeches. The site's name, The Percentage of Truth, refers to the rankings they give while evaluating politicians' claims.

Among its successes was a 2016 report where it fact-checked a claim by Erdogan that Turkey was now a "high-income country" according to the OECD. The site revealed that the OECD still considered Turkey a middle-income country and had predicted that it "could become" a high-income country in 2030. Erdogan stopped making the claim after Doğruluk Payı's report.

"This helped us understand our impact. Probably, his advisers were following our content,"said Kaplica.

Six months after Doğruluk Payı's launch, pro-government groups came up with similar initiatives. "They focused on foreign news coverage of Turkey. Theirs was politically motivated analysis, not fact-checking," said Kaplıca.

Then, in 2016, came Teyit (Verify), a Turkish verification platform that analyses the accuracy of dubious content published on the web. Its founder, Mehmet Atakan Foça, is a 31-year-old journalist and social entrepreneur.

"Between 2015 and 2017, there were numerous bomb attacks in Turkey, and we saw how people were victimised by misinformation," he told Index. "Anger, panic and sudden strong emotional shifts showed how quickly misinformation could spread, and how people could believe it."

In approaching pro-government "fact-checking" initiatives, Foça recommends taking them with a pinch

of salt. "They've many shortcomings in transparency – from how they analyse suspect information to ... their methodology," he said. "They're little more than tools for disseminating one side's views. Meanwhile, fact-checking requires a strong methodology, equal treatment of all sides, acting independently, and transparency in all things, including sources of revenue."

In describing "the great methodological differences" between the government's Disinformation Bulletins and the activities at Teyit, Foça said: "We adhere to criteria like importance, urgency, prevalence; we use open sources, whereas the Disinformation Bulletin treats the statements of government officials as truth."

According to the Reuters Institute Digital News Report, only 36% of news consumers in Turkey trust their accuracy. Foça said people chose Teyit to get their information as trust in the media was so low. Can the Centre for Combatting Disinformation achieve trust?

"While disinformation is a serious problem that can be solved with long-term planning and changing policies, the Disinformation Law offers the destructive path of punishment," Foça said. "We'll see how it's implemented in practice and its effects in the coming days. But this isn't the way to solve the problem."

Koray Kaplıca is worried that "fake news" listed in the Disinformation Bulletin may lead ordinary people to end up in prison. "This will become a headache, especially in the run-up to the election campaign," he said.

Another concern for Kaplıca and his fellow fact-checkers is attacks by government-funded groups who can now act in an official capacity.

"They attack us when we fact-check LGBTQI issues," he said. "They share links to our content in their Telegram channels, and the troll attacks begin. They also target our work on women's rights and industrial disasters." There were similar attacks when Kaplıca and his team began fact-checking speeches in 2014, but those were less coordinated. He had no concerns for his safety eight years ago but admits he would have today if they were only just starting up Doğruluk Payı. And he wonders whether Turkish pollsters will be allowed to post their findings in the run-up to the election because of the new law.

The law, passed so close to next summer's presidential elections, is dangerous, according to Karakaş.

"Normally, when I report a piece, readers can dispute its details and come up with opposing arguments," she said. "But the Disinformation Bulletin is announcing the 'official truth' on a matter and says, 'This is how this happened, end of story'. It is a way of showing the stick to people." This has had an impact on her interviewees.

"They withdraw their statements after interviews. They even change specific words. Others refuse to talk altogether," she said. But she insists it won't affect her journalism.

"I'll keep on doing my reporting. Just because they passed this law, I won't stop writing my articles." ✖

Kaya Genç is Turkey's contributing editor for Index. He is based in Istanbul

"They focused on foreign news coverage of Turkey. Theirs was politically motivated analysis, not fact-checking," said Kaplıca

51(04):27/29|DOI:10.1177/03064220221144881

Reaching for an emotional flak jacket

Discussing their own mental health has long been taboo for journalists. **RACHAEL JOLLEY** explores why and asks whether anything has changed

RETURNING FROM A war zone can be jarring for journalists – a fact Peter Wilson knows all too well.

"It's really difficult to adjust when you haven't got a life-or-death decision, and you're not seeing horrible things every minute," said Wilson, former news and Europe editor of The Australian.

One day he was covering the tennis at Wimbledon; the next, the war in Iraq. In 2003, Wilson, his photographer and a translator hired a car in Kuwait and drove across the Iraqi border. They were captured by soldiers about a week later.

"Initially, they thought we were spies and eventually we convinced them we were journalists," Wilson remembered. "It was terrifying.

"There are literally tanks blowing up around us and we're in a sort of SUV. It felt like it was made out of plastic because it was kind of bouncing around the road with the shockwaves of explosions. So, it was a pretty long and hairy drive," Wilson told Index.

Wilson then spent time reporting from Baghdad. When a fellow journalist was seriously injured by mortar fire, he used his basic first aid, but the reporter died before reaching hospital.

Back in London, where he was based, Wilson was offered some time off to write a book about his experience, and he feels that helped him cope.

Now 61, he said that in those days there was little preparation for any mental health consequences on reporters or their teams – nor any expectation that they might need specific counselling to prepare themselves before heading off to cover a conflict. He remembers some colleagues and other journalists did have problems after difficult assignments and it was not handled well.

"It was considered your fault that you had a bit of an issue or if you couldn't sleep, or you're drinking too much, or your marriage broke up afterwards."

But he feels things have changed.

"I would hope that if I was the news editor doing that today I'd be a little bit more aware of the vulnerability and what's at stake for that person, and that there could be lifelong damage," he said.

There are some signs that taboos around mental health issues stemming from covering difficult and dangerous stories are starting to be lifted – at least a little – but not for every reporter in every situation.

Ela Stapley worked in Mexico as a journalist until 2016 and is now a digital security consultant for media organisations, based in the UK. She said she doesn't know any journalists

> It was considered your fault that you had a bit of an issue or if you couldn't sleep, or you were drinking too much, or your marriage broke up

ABOVE: A journalist takes cover during shelling in Horenka, Ukraine on 7 March 2022

in Mexico who haven't been held at gunpoint or threatened with a knife at some point, because so many stories have a link to organised crime.

"The trauma impact for them was very high, whether they would realise that or not, or admit that or not," she said. "I left Mexico because I just couldn't do it anymore."

And she thinks newsrooms are still well behind on mental health support for journalists.

Hannah Storm, co-director of the Headlines Network, runs mental health training for newsrooms.

"I don't think even now there's still really sufficient conversations around how you support people going into difficult and dangerous places," she said.

The trauma impact for them was very high, whether they would realise that or not

Storm worked as a journalist in post-conflict and environmental disaster zones including Haiti and Libya. In 1999 there were conversations about flak jackets but no real discussions about dealing with the emotional problems caused by working in hostile environments. "You were just expected to have a few drinks and get over it," she said. Along with taking the right kit, she believes there needs to be emotional and psychological support as well.

Stuart Ramsay, the longest serving foreign correspondent for the UK's Sky News, recently told the podcast Behind the Headlines with Headlines Network about being shot on assignment in Ukraine, and how he copes with the stress. He talked about how he decompresses after coming back from an overseas assignment.

"Everyone deals with things very differently," he said. "One thing is not to go on the lash the minute you get back. Control the partying. And do mundane things."

Sarah Ward-Lilley, who was managing editor of news at the BBC until 2021 and head of the BBC's international bureaux, said trauma and PTSD awareness started to be built into the organisation's hostile environment training about 20 years ago.

"We started saying, 'Look, these can also have an effect on you emotionally. It's not unusual to feel this, please look out for each other.' Acute reactions can be quite powerful. But they are your normal reactions to abnormal events," she said. But she acknowledges there has been resistance along the way from the journalists themselves.

"There is a feeling that if I am struggling in any way to do any of this story, or any of this work, I'll never get sent on the big story again," she said.

Recent research from Middlesex University found that UK journalists felt newsroom culture and supervisors' lack of understanding "were obstacles". Researchers said that, until recently, any discussion of emotions appeared "to be at odds with the principles of the profession". There were widely held perceptions in the media that being a journalist involved "having a thick skin" and "being able to cope".

In the early days of the Covid-19 pandemic in Europe, when cases were rocketing in Italy, Milan-based freelance journalist Alessio Perrone was inundated with commissions from UK and US newsdesks to report on how the virus was spreading. He remembers talking to families about loved ones who had died and one funeral director saying that mass graves were being dug.

"I would work from 7am to 10pm – it was the busiest period of my life," Perrone said. "In some ways work was a distraction and helped me cope."

Then a friend got in touch and suggested talking to a therapist, and he was able to share his experiences. He said getting support became really important.

"It doesn't feel like a taboo. I don't know if it's a generational thing. But I'm surrounded by people that I could talk to about these things." ✖

Rachael Jolley is a lecturer in journalism at Cardiff University, and former editor-in-chief at Index

51(04):30/31|DOI:10.1177/03064220221144882

Bad seeds

The activist **VANDANA SHIVA**, who has spent her life advocating for biodiversity and battling corporations that push genetically modified organisms, comments on how the control of seeds silences farmers in India

SEED IS LIVING. Seed is the source of life. Seed is memory and the future.

The ability of farmers to grow and exchange seed has long been the basis of maintaining both biodiversity and food security. Seeds are the first link in the food chain – the means of food production and agricultural livelihoods. This freedom is how both farming communities and nature express themselves.

Today, nature and culture's freedom to evolve, to express themselves freely, is under violent and direct threat. Suppressing seed freedom impacts the very fabric of human life and the life of the planet.

For millions of years, seed has evolved to give us the diversity and richness of life. For thousands of years, farmers, especially women, have bred seed together. They've worked with nature to further increase the diversity that it gave us and adapt it to the needs of different cultures. Biodiversity and cultural diversity have mutually shaped one another, allowing cultural expression to flourish.

But industrial agriculture, based on chemical monocultures where land is filled with a single plant, has silenced the diversity of seed. Out of thousands of available species, today we largely depend on just 12 globally traded crops.

As well as silencing diversity through monocultures and uniformity, in the past few decades there has been another attempt to halt the evolution of seed. Sterile terminator crops have been created which do not produce their own seeds. Patents have also been imposed.

Farmers lose their freedom to speak, their freedom to live, under this seed totalitarianism. The fact that farmers in India are driven to suicide illustrates that all doors to speaking their pain and seeking justice are closed to them.

In 1987, I was invited to a meeting organised by NGO the Dag Hammarskjöld Foundation on new biotechnologies, where major chemical corporations were present. They said they were not making enough profits through chemicals and needed to genetically engineer seeds so they could apply patents to them. Every farmer would have to buy seeds from them every season.

During the follow-up conference at the UN in Geneva, I first heard of the General Agreement on Tariffs and Trade, which became the World Trade Organization. Its Trade Related Aspects of Intellectual Property Rights agreement opened the door for multinational corporations to enter countries such as India and try to introduce genetically modified organisms and patents on seed.

That is when I committed myself to protect our seed diversity and farmers' rights to save, breed and exchange seed freely.

A patent on seeds means that these living organisms are defined as

> **Farmers lose their freedom to speak, their freedom to live, under this seed totalitarianism**

something manufactured, invented by a corporation. Patents on seeds are a censorship of seed freedom. They halt evolution and the freedom of farmers to save, share and co-evolve seed.

For me, this is unscientific. Seeds are self-organised, self-evolving, self-renewing, self-multiplying living systems. A seed is not a machine. A patent on seeds is unjust and unethical. Now, four giants control the majority of the world's commercial seed supply. They are Bayer (which acquired Monsanto),

CREDIT: Joerg Boethling/Alamy

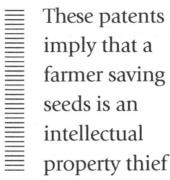

These patents imply that a farmer saving seeds is an intellectual property thief

website, where I used to publish my research, was hacked not once but twice.

Scientists who carry out independent research on GMOs have been silenced, too, beginning with Dr Arpad Putztai, a leading plant lectin expert based in the UK. His career was ended after a controversial episode where he attempted to share research about the toxic effect of GM potatoes on rats.

Where the freedom of seeds disappears, so too does the freedom of farmers. This is why we started the movement for Earth democracy, Navdanya. The name means "Nine Seeds", which symbolises the richness of biodiversity. Movements such as Navdanya allow for the possibility of a different future. They shape laws that defend the integrity of seed and farmers' rights, based on ethics, ecology and diversity.

Since 1987, we have worked for the defence of seed sovereignty and seed freedom by creating community seed banks. These protect seeds and the freedom of farmers to save and exchange seed. They lift the censorship imposed by patents and intellectual property rights and halt the erasure of diversity. They are the archives of freedom in nature and culture, repositories of Indigenous knowledge. They create hope and give life. ✖

Vandana Shiva is an Indian eco-activist, author and scholar. Her most recent book is Terra Viva, published by Chelsea Green

Corteva, ChemChina and BASF. These patents imply that a farmer saving seeds is an intellectual property thief. But it means more. A system in which seed has become a corporate monopoly, a system in which a few companies control the seed supply, is in effect a system of slavery for farmers. It silences knowledge and freedom. It even costs farmers' lives.

Seed slavery has trapped farmers in debt. The high number of suicides has long been a cause for concern in India,

and in 2021 alone more than 10,000 people involved in farming took their own lives.

When I heard about farmers' suicides, I started to monitor the government data and work in the field. I wrote and talked about the farmers' plights, but then the censorship started. I used to have columns in Indian newspapers, but pressure was put on the news organisations to silence me - I cannot say from whom. When I appeared on TV, the channels were threatened. My

51(04):32/33|DOI:10.1177/03064220221144883

Singapore's elastic band of a Public Order Act

If you're in with the government, protest away. If you're not, forget about it or face consequences. **KIRSTEN HAN** argues that the law is being increasingly flexed in all the wrong ways

STANDING OUTSIDE THE State Court of Singapore, just beyond the steps at the entrance, Jolovan Wham held up a piece of A4 paper on which he'd printed the words "Drop the charges against Terry Xu and Daniel de Costa". A friend snapped a photo for him on a mobile phone, Wham put away the sign, then entered the courtroom to attend the hearing involving the friends he'd named. The whole thing took about 15 seconds.

That was 2018. Four years later, Wham would serve a 15-day prison sentence (in lieu of a £1,900 fine) just for doing that.

In 2009, Singapore's Parliament passed the Public Order Act, a sweeping piece of legislation that effectively criminalised protests held in public spaces. Under the law, the term

"assembly" is defined very broadly as a meeting or gathering to demonstrate support for, or opposition to, particular views or actions, or to publicise causes or commemorate events.

This applies even to actions involving only one person, making Singapore a special place where individuals are not able to "assemble" alone. Although it is technically possible to apply for a police permit to protest in public, activists are usually unsuccessful. The only exception to this rule is Speakers' Corner, a

CREDIT: Edgar Su/Reuters/Alamy

BELOW: Human rights activist Jolovan Wham (left) arrives at the State Court in Singapore in February 2019 after being arrested for a 15-second peaceful protest

modest-sized park near the central business district where Singaporeans can gather for a cause (subject to conditions, of course) without prior permission.

A little over a week after Wham finished his prison stint, the Attorney-General's Chambers (AGC) – who had argued so determinedly for Wham's conviction – announced that they would not be taking action against ruling party parliamentarian Louis Ng for posing with hawkers running food stalls while holding up a piece of A4 paper saying "Support Them" alongside a smiley face.

According to the prosecutors, Ng had merely been "expressing care and support" for hawkers during the pandemic. The nature of the act and the intention, the AGC's spokesman told the press, were key to deciding if it would be in the public interest to prosecute.

It must have been obvious that comparisons between Wham and Ng's cases would be made, because the prosecution was also quick to distinguish between the two cases. They'd gone after Wham, they said, because he had been standing in a restricted area (outside the State Court).

What wasn't addressed was that the AGC had also charged Wham for taking a photo on a public street while holding a piece of cardboard with a smiley face drawn on it. Although the AGC did eventually withdraw that case, the fact remains that they had initially thought it in the public interest to prosecute him for it. There had been no benefit of the doubt for Wham, no "he was just expressing care" rationale.

Even if we consider the AGC's argument that the area around the State Court is a permanently restricted area in which no one will ever be allowed to demonstrate – itself an unjustified restriction of the right to freedom of assembly – prosecuting someone for standing with a sign just long enough to snap a photo is a ludicrous stretch of a law aimed at public order. Surveillance footage played during Wham's trial showed that, apart from the friend

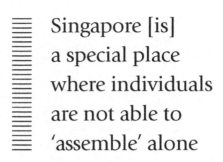

Singapore [is] a special place where individuals are not able to 'assemble' alone

taking the photo, no one had even noticed his presence.

It also doesn't always seem to have been a problem. Years ago, I watched activists unfurl a banner in front of the press outside the State Courts and no action had been taken against them for that. Insisting that such an action falls under the definition of "illegal assembly" is a weaponisation of the Public Order Act to suppress fundamental rights to assembly and expression, and it seems like the state is now much more willing to wield this weapon.

Law enforcement can quickly turn political. If actions aligned with establishment messages are excused, even though they could fall under the Public Order Act's wide definition, while actions that critique the powerful are deemed "protests" no matter how small or brief, then what Singaporeans are being told is that only acts that challenge the state will be penalised.

This is the danger of over-broad legislation. It's also a modus operandi of the Singapore government – introduce laws that are widely scoped and give the authorities maximum discretion in application. In this way, the authorities can be presented with two people harmlessly holding up signs and decide one was simply being a nice guy while the other had threatened public order. ✖

Kirsten Han is a Singaporean independent journalist running the newsletter We, The Citizens, *and a member of the Transformative Justice Collective*

51(04):34/35|DOI:10.1177/03064220221144884

Hong Kong's valiants with a message for the world

Exiled Hong Kong protester **YEUNG WILLIE SAU** is making it his mission to record the stories of other exiled protesters. But the stakes couldn't be higher

EUNG WILLIE SAU (a pseudonym) is more than an anonymous participant in Hong Kong's democracy movement. He has also acted as an interviewer and used his writing to record the fight and flight of Hong Kong protesters during 2019. His book, Clandestine in Hong Kong, lets the world hear the voices of those young people who stood at the front line of the fight against totalitarianism. But the simple act of publishing it has seen himself and those connected to it harassed and charged with violating Hong Kong's National Security Law. Still, as Sau tells Index, he will not be silenced.

Since the eruption of the anti-extradition law movement in June 2019, Sau has participated in the movement's support and supply operations, and has come to know many of the frontline protesters. After he left Hong Kong, he continued to support those protesters, who are both in Hong Kong and overseas.

He firmly believes in the French author Milan Kundera's philosophy that "the struggle of man against power is the struggle of memory against forgetting". So when the Chinese government forcibly implemented the National Security Law, shutting down media, arresting elected members of the legislative council, starting massive internet investigations, and even arresting the author of a children's picture book that depicted the protest movement, Sau decided to join forces with Aegis, a Taiwanese organisation that provides support to Hong Kong protesters.

In 2020 he started to interview different frontline "valiants" (as some of the protesters are known) who had fled overseas, and he began chronicling their journeys. Sau spent more than a year communicating with this group of young

political exiles, trying to understand how some of them who never cared for or understood politics in the past went from attending Korean-popstar concerts to picking up petrol bombs to fight the communist regime on the streets.

From April 2021, he started to post his interviews and stories on his Patreon page, with all the earnings donated to Aegis, as a way to support the livelihoods and education of the young political exiles in Taiwan. Later, he put these reports into a collective work, Clandestine in Hong Kong: The Unfinished Journey of The Valiant, an extract of which is published here.

He originally planned to publish in early 2022 in Taiwan, but this was delayed due to constant suppression from the Chinese government. For example, when the book was being printed, Sau's team members were harassed and intimidated by unknown people, through phone calls and visits. Their families were threatened and they were told they would face severe consequences if the book was ever published. This caused some team members to resign out of fear.

Still, Sau carried on, and found new partners. Finally, this June, the book was translated into Japanese and published. It was then published independently in Taiwan in its original Chinese form. Almost immediately, those behind it were charged under the National Security Law.

It's little wonder that Sau continues to write anonymously. But he also continues to help the exiled valiants, unwilling to let the threats stop him. He told Index: "For my own safety, I have remained anonymous, and I hope to continue to do so. At the same time, I would like to continue to publish my writings, just like graffiti artist Banksy. I'm just an ordinary Hongkonger who wants to let people from different cultures around the world know how young people in Hong Kong are at the forefront of the global fight against the totalitarian Chinese communist regime."

LEFT: More than one million protested the controversial Extradition Bill in Hong Kong, 2019

What? My daughter is a rioter?

"I REALLY LIKE [singer] Kary Ng's The Motto. I also like Break Up Ruthlessly. Among the kids in my dad's circle of friends, I'm the eldest. I was born when my parents were young. I don't have many friends in my age group. Dad loves getting together with his friends. He always brought me along to hang out with uncles and aunties. They often give me 'chicken soup for the soul' and advice about life. Mom's friends are mostly single women, so I'd go with them to karaoke, mostly singing songs of their generation. When I got older, I began to understand Kary Ng's lyrics. And since I'm a nostalgic type, I'm used to listening to old pop tunes."

To me, Kary Ng belongs to a new generation of Hong Kong pop singers. But for 17-year-old Jingjing (a pseudonym), Ng is an ageing pop star.

Jingjing maintains she's a normal girl growing up in a normal family. Life is normal. But because she's an only child, her parents are strict. She was enrolled in a Band 1 secondary school. On school days, she must return home by 7 or 8pm. She made a point in telling me that after her exile, her school had been demoted to Band 3.

"We can't exclude that I was the reason. As soon as I left, the school's academic scores tumbled."

Her parents didn't believe in giving her much pocket money, since that would offer a means to go around town. She only had $300 per week, which also covered breakfast and lunch. Since the cheapest breakfast and lunch would add up to $50, she'd have at most $50 of spare cash per week. For that reason, she rarely went out during weekends. She might meet with friends once or twice a month, hanging out at the Kwai Fong Shopping Mall. She rarely spent money to buy speciality gear for her favourite online games. She was a typical, rather obedient type, yet her life was shattered by the protests.

"I've always been involved in inter-school activities, organising balls etc. In July, a senior female student suggested setting up a concern group, and I organised one with three girls and two boys from my class. Our campus concern group took part in the protests. At that time, I told Mum I was joining friends to shout some slogans, hang up some posters. I didn't dare mention 'dog taunting' [dogs being what Hong Kong protesters came to call the police], and of course I couldn't tell her that I belonged to an actual team."

Jingjing normally helped with putting up posters. During protests, she'd assist in supply stations. Veteran protesters would teach her hand signs and how to transport provisions. "When we retreat, we only take the important things, such as small-sized bottled water, because they are easy to move and store for later use. We'd leave the large bottles (three or four litres), because you can't carry them and run. We must carry saline solution, 'pig snouts' [respirator masks] and goggles, because they are expensive."

Jingjing would bring these supplies back home, hiding them in her bedroom closet.

Once her mother asked about them, and she made the excuse that other people couldn't bring them home, so she was storing them temporarily. But her mother wasn't that gullible. Every time Jingjing went out she'd be clad in black, carrying a big backpack, so her mother couldn't help but ask.

"At that point she found out. 'What? My daughter is a rioter? You have to run? Dogs run after you?' From that moment on, they forbade me to go out."

Outing for lamb stew, with a dash of teargas

"Basically, my parents both belong to the yellow camp. Mum is more yellow [the colour associated with supporting the protesters]. Dad is a driver. As long as his job isn't impacted, he doesn't care about anything. But many of our relatives are blue [the colour associated with supporting the police], so my parents try their best not to express their views in their company or else there'll be family feuds. We live in the New Territories, and have friends from the walled villages. During July 21, even my parents were persuaded to believe the story that white-clad men were 'protecting their homeland'. By 31 August, when my parents saw news coverage of the police rushing into [Mass Transit Railway] train compartments at Prince Edward Station and beating people up, they screamed obscenities at the television. I was very angry and scolded them: 'What are you doing swearing at the television? Come out and help next time!'

"Do you remember the follow-up incident in Yuen Long in September? Friends belonging to the campus concern group all came. They asked why I didn't join them. In the end, my parents came out with me; it was like a family outing. After we got there, they went into Mushroom [a Hong Kong-style diner], sat down and ordered a lamb stew. I went to see my mates to check if I could help. I was on the other side of the main street while my parents were two or three streets away. Later on, to avoid the police, I ran into the park. At that point I got a call from Mum. She said the police had been firing teargas, she was eating her lamb stew but her eyes were burning. Dad was worried so he ran out to look for me. That was the first time Mum inhaled teargas. I told her, 'Use the saline solution I gave you to rinse your mouth and wash your eye.' Guess what? She told me she left it at home. I was upset, I'd given her provisions for emergencies, yet she didn't bring them along? I was yelling at her on the phone: 'Weren't you supposed to help? You ordered a lamb stew, and now you need a first-aider?' In the end, I had no choice but to leave my friends for Mum.

"After the teargas attack, Mum was very weak, so I had to keep her company. We went to an upstairs private bar owned by one of my parents' friends. When they saw what happened to her, they reprimanded me for exposing her to danger. I admit I was a bit extreme then. I screamed back, accusing them that they just found easy ways such as eating in 'yellow establishments' to redeem themselves, as if that was already participating in a protest. Who's going to save Hong Kong? Precisely because you didn't fight, uncles and

ABOVE: Young protesters construct a barricade in Hong Kong in 2019

aunties, my generation has suffered so. We asked you to join us in the general strike, but you didn't. You didn't want to stand on the street to hang up posters, to help share something. What have you done for Hong Kong?

"I swore at these uncles and they yelled back at me, that I should just help put up posters and not stand on the frontlines in these protests. I couldn't stand it, I told them that if they wanted to, they would've done it a long time ago; they didn't need to teach me now. Finally, I broke down in tears. At this time, a more restrained uncle told me that they were also yellow. But to make a living, they can't just strike whenever they want to. But during off-hours, they'd sent provisions to the protest sites, even driving young protesters from place to place. Only then did I realise that among these uncles and aunties were some 'hidden yellow' folks helping those in the frontlines.

"After that night, my parents' attitude changed. They started to donate money, eat in yellow establishments. But the biggest change was that they no longer stopped me from going out. Of course, they wished that whenever I was in a protest, I could send them a message telling them where I was, assuring them that I was safe." ✖

Yeung Willie Sau is a Hong Kong activist

51(04):36/39|DOI:10.1177/03064220221144885

Press under pressure

Media freedom in Italy was always weak, but the new far-right government is attacking it with renewed vigour, writes **ALESSIO PERRONE**

A FEW DAYS BEFORE the late-September election that would consign power to the hard right Fratelli d'Italia (Brothers of Italy) and a coalition of allies, giving Italy its most right-wing government since Benito Mussolini, John Martin's phone pinged with a notification.

Martin, a freelance journalist who covers Italy for publications in the UK and the USA and has asked Index not to use his real name, had just written an article about the party's programme,

quoting experts on both sides of the political divide. Here was the bite-back.

A party spokesperson criticised Martin's use of the term "far-right", which they called "slanderous", and in the ensuing conversation asked him to change the article's headline, or else there would be consequences for his newspaper.

"I wonder if I'll be more careful about the way I present certain news items," he said of the event. "And if, more subtly, this behaviour will influence the way I report the facts."

Martin had already covered four Italian governments, and occasionally politicians would complain to him that they weren't given enough space in stories, but it was the first time one was pressuring him so overtly.

"I didn't see this as intimidation, more as a difference of opinions," he told Index. "But it became clear how the party strived to control the narrative, using very direct methods."

It wasn't an isolated event. On

It became clear how the party strived to control the narrative

OPPOSITE: Giorgia Meloni campaigning during regional elections in Piacenza, Italy in January 2020

the campaign trail and in office, Prime Minister Giorgia Meloni, her government, MPs and supporters have already picked several fights with critical media organisations and individual reporters – some small, others serious enough to have observers worried about freedom of speech in the country.

"The situation was already very uncertain before the new government," said Giuseppe Giulietti, president of the National Federation of the Italian Press. "Now it's even more uncertain."

Italy's unflattering track record on press freedom predates Meloni's government. The country has long failed to improve the independence of public broadcasting service Rai, introduce conflict of interest rules or reform its libel laws – in Italy, defamation through the media is a criminal offence that carries prison sentences of up to three years, and defamation lawsuits are regularly used to intimidate journalists.

Some 9,479 defamation proceedings were initiated against journalists in 2017 alone, the last year for which data from the National Statistics Institute is available, but 60% were dismissed while only 6.6% went to trial. Months before September's election, Reporters Without Borders ranked Italy 58th in its 2022 world press freedom index – the lowest spot in western Europe.

"The [lack of interest] toward press freedom has unfortunately been going on for a long time and under governments of many colours," Giulietti said, comparing previous governments' inaction on press freedom to "leaving loaded guns on the table".

He added: "The situation is obviously destined to get worse. The prime minister and her government have already entered into conflicts with journalists repeatedly."

In late August, young supporters followed and filmed journalists at Meloni's first campaign speech as they asked her supporters questions about fascism. When Meloni was sworn in as prime minister, she refused to drop any defamation charges against reporters, unlike several previous prime ministers. She is suing anti-mafia journalist Roberto Saviano, who has been living under police protection since 2006 for his investigations into organised crime. When daily newspaper Domani published an investigation into her defence minister Guido Crosetto's ties to arms manufacturers, he did not respond to the paper's allegations but instead publicly threatened to sue it for libel.

Meloni has expressed admiration for Hungarian Prime Minister Viktor Orbán's work, and has even adopted similar rhetoric in her speech against the "globalist elites" allegedly conspiring to bring down conservative values. In a message delivered to a right-wing rally organised by Spain's far-right party Vox in October 2022, where speakers included Donald Trump, Orbán and Polish Prime Minister Mateusz Morawiecki, Meloni listed the things that come under attack by the "globalist mainstream", including the family, religion, borders, labour and freedom of expression, the erosion of which she blamed on "cancel culture" by "the dictatorship of the politically correct".

Sergio Scandura, who is at the forefront of reporting on migration in the Mediterranean Sea for Radio Radicale, said the climate in Italy was already "Orbánist". He said much of the damage was done by previous governments, who restricted journalists' access to the field, keeping them tens of metres away from docking NGO rescue boats and police operations in ports, and therefore preventing them from documenting the arrivals. Official sources also increasingly refuse to divulge "sensitive" information.

"The story of asylum seekers is treated as a state secret," he said.

But the "silencer" effect around

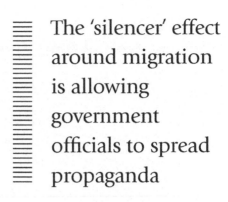

The 'silencer' effect around migration is allowing government officials to spread propaganda

migration is allowing government officials to spread propaganda, such as blaming NGO search and rescue operations in the Mediterranean for asylum seeker arrivals.

In the weeks after the election, the attacks against "globalist elites" were increasingly directed towards the press and freedom of expression. In subsequent statements, Crosetto called critical reporting "international defamation to weaken the country". Meloni went on the record saying that "a whole part of Italy is working against Italy". And her culture minister, Gennaro Sangiuliano, complained about the left's "cultural hegemony" and said he supported funding more right-wing films and TV shows.

When daily newspaper La Repubblica ran an article debunking the government narrative around migration, Claudio Borghi, a senator in the coalition government, tweeted that there were "crooked and collaborationists infiltrated everywhere" and that "the press is totally in the hands of the enemies of the homeland".

It's too early to tell how this pressure will impact reporters. After the episode he was involved with, Martin reached out to his newsroom in the UK, which decided not to change the headline at the behest of Fratelli d'Italia. ✖

Alessio Perrone is a freelance journalist based in Italy

51(04):40/41|DOI:10.1177/03064220221144886

PICTURED:
A protester records the action during a Black Lives Matter rally in 2020

Radical timelines

It has been 25 years since the first recognised social media company was launched. Little known today, SixDegrees combined popular features such as profiles, lists of friends and university affiliations in one service and amassed millions of followers before it closed its doors in 2000.

Facebook, coming fast on its heels, changed the game and did what social media has been heralded for – creating connections in the millions, nay billions.

Today, according to the latest Facebook figures, the company has almost three billion registered active monthly users. TikTok meanwhile, which launched only in 2017, is thought to have reached one billion active users by the end of 2022.

The power of social media to give a voice to the unheard and ignite social change is undeniable. But of course there is the darker side, from bots to trolls. We've kept an eye on both sides of the story over the last quarter of a century.

Now we've asked four journalists, **LILI RUTAI, MEHRAN BHAT, MUQEET SHAH** and **ANDREW MAMBONDIYANI**, to explore social media in their countries.

In many ways they couldn't be more different, and yet similar threads run through the fabric of their digital landscapes. Has social media been a help or a hindrance? We'll let you decide.

Hungarians face off on Facebook

LILI RUTAI unpicks the media landscape in Hungary, where in the absence of much independent press, citizens turn to news on Facebook, which can be a breeding ground for propaganda

HUNGARIAN PRIME MINISTER Viktor Orbán has been called many things, including a "dictator" by European Commission president Jean-Claude Juncker and a "press freedom predator" by Reporters Without Borders (RSF).

The latest media outlet to fall victim to the right-wing Fidesz party government is Klubrádió, one of the last remaining independent radio stations, which ceased broadcasting in February after its licence was revoked. Streaming continues online, however, giving a platform to critics of Orbán.

Perhaps the most visible event in the suppression of the free press was in July 2020. More than 10,000 people took to the streets of Budapest in a protest against the crackdown on Index, one of Hungary's most-read newspapers. The majority of the editorial team left when government-friendly actors took ownership.

According to RSF, the government currently controls more than 80% of the media – including most local papers, public television and radio channels – and is expanding. At the same time that the government has taken hold of it, trust in the media has decreased. Reuters research suggests that the majority of Hungarians now get their news from the internet, including social media, where influencers and channels take over the power vacuum left by the lack of reliable media.

One such new medium is Partizán, a YouTube channel founded by activist and director Márton Gulyás in 2018. After interviewing the joint opposition's prime ministerial candidate Péter Márki-Zay, as well as creating livestreams on current events, Partizán has almost 300,000 subscribers. Jakab Tóth, a presenter at Partizán, told

Index that many people viewed it as a new, independent medium.

"I think it says a lot about the press that an openly leftist channel, which by chance isn't connected to a party, is seen as public broadcasting," he said.

Partizán broadcasts on YouTube, but Hungary's most populated social media platform is Facebook, with around 75% of the population registered and 60% getting their news there.

But Facebook isn't a fair playground. Ahead of the 2022 election, when Orbán held on to power, a government-friendly institute supporting Christian conservative voices – Megafon – spent more than a billion forints (around $2.5 million) on adverts with Facebook influencers repeating the government's lines. They were presented in an accessible way for social media users: plastered with emojis.

"Previously, the traditional press held the role of a guardian," Blanka Zöldi, the editor-in-chief of Lakmusz, a fact-checking website in Hungary, said.

"The editors and journalists judged which information that reached them was →

> ≡ The majority of the editorial team left when government-friendly actors took ownership

The government currently controls more than 80% of the media – including most local papers, public television and radio

→ genuine, trustworthy, and these ended up in the magazines, so readers encountered them. On social media, there are no such guards."

In relation to the war in Ukraine, she said: "The most prominent experts in Russia used their Facebook to inform, but the wildest conspiracy theorists ... had the same platform."

In Hungary, the risk of propaganda is the same.

"I think that if someone has the potential to reach masses, they must use it for building, not destroying," Bettina Tóth, a supporter of the ruling right-wing Fidesz party and a social media influencer, told Index. Previously a participant in a talent show, she decided to get into politics when, due to an illness, she had to quit singing. She joined Fidesz's youth organisation, Fidelitas, and has amassed a large following on both Facebook and TikTok.

Tóth posts viral trends and short explanations of current events, including the election, poking fun at Fidesz's opposition. Her Facebook cover image is a montage of pictures of her with Fidesz politicians.

Despite her stance being clear, some users view her as part of the media. "It's just like I'm watching the news programme," one commenter said under her rendering of a case of revenge porn, complemented with two smiley emojis. In Hungary's battle for truth those emojis might fool some people – but not all.

Lili Rutai is a Hungarian freelance journalist. She has worked with Vice, Radio Free Europe and The Independent

The disappearing tweeters of Kashmir

MEHRAN BHAT and **MUQEET SHAH** report on the intimidation from Kashmiri authorities that silences social media users

IN KASHMIR, SOME social media users have gone into virtual hiding. Others dare not write anything political.

Ever since the repeal of a law giving Jammu and Kashmir special status, the authorities in the conflict-torn region have tightened their grip on what is said online. The fear is palpable among those who use social media and now avoid criticising authorities or sharing their opinions online, fearing reprisal. Many people, including government employees who have to submit details of their accounts to the police, have deleted their social media accounts permanently to keep themselves safe.

"Four Kashmiri journalists are in jail, a journalist friend of mine was booked under a controversial law for his reportage and I have been detained twice for my journalism," Qazi Shibli, editor-in-chief of local news portal The Kashmiriyat, told Index. "Journalists are being summoned for what they write to their social media. If this is not curbing of your democratic freedom, then nothing in the world is."

In July 2020, Shibli was interrogated by the cyber police, before being detained for the second time. Frontline Defenders, an international human rights organisation founded in Dublin, reported that he was "being targeted for his documentation of the lives of those living in Kashmir". In 2019, he was sentenced to nine months in prison for a tweet about troops in the region.

There are more examples of the silencing effect of social media censorship. In December 2021, a bank employee was suspended from her job in Kashmir for reacting with a laughing emoji to a Facebook post which announced the death of Indian defence chief Bipin Rawat. Her employers deemed the emoji a derogatory remark.

On 14 August 2020, news website The Kashmir Walla first reported the digital disappearance of social media users in Kashmir. Many young Twitter and other social media users in Kashmir were summoned by the cyber police, and although they were released after questioning, it added to the climate of fear.

"You have to understand there's a proper mechanism in Kashmir and a team of authorities is constantly observing your

social media presence," claimed Asrar Syed, a 20-year-old man from Srinagar.

"If by chance something you've posted doesn't favour [the government] or [criticism of] authorities comes under their scanner, you'll be picked up in a night raid and booked."

He said many people today were behind bars because they had criticised the regime. Their families are suffering and their careers are also at stake.

"My close ones have often told me to delete my Twitter handle and stop writing anything. I still cannot choose silence because that's what this regime wants – to silence us with fear," Syed said. He still wants to speak the truth, even though living under restrictions and surveillance in Kashmir has taken a mental toll.

According to a report in 2020 by news site Article 14, the then superintendent of police, Tahir Ashraf Bhatti, who was also the head of the cyber cell, said that the questioning "has nothing to do with politics and is not based on political lines". He denied that the police were silencing dissent.

ABOVE: Men on their phones after internet was restored in Kashmir, 2019

"The way censorship has grown in the recent past is worrying," Shibli said. "There is an intermittent investigation of what the state has called the 'Ecosystem of Narrative Terrorism'."

According to local news reports, the investigation he refers to involves raking through an individual's body of work.

Shibli said journalists braving this age of extreme intimidation are profiled along with activists, lawyers, academics and others, with police labelling some content as anti-national. Then the process of scrutiny, summons, intimidation and jailing begins.

According to Shibli, the fear that gripped Kashmir after the targeting of social media users is gripping the land more firmly and its impact is now felt more than ever.

Mehran Bhat and *Muqeet Shah* are *freelance journalists based in Kashmir*

Zimbabwe's new hope

Opposition voices are at risk in Zimbabwe, but could social media offer a space for dissent? ANDREW MAMBONDIYANI speaks to activists in the country

THE RUN-UP TO Zimbabwe's 2023 election has been marred by crackdowns on journalists, political opponents and human rights activists. Under president Emmerson Mnangagwa's regime, dissenting voices are increasingly being silenced in print and broadcast media. Of the few remaining "independent" radio stations, most are owned or heavily controlled by Mnangagwa's cronies. However, platforms such as Twitter, Facebook and WhatsApp are giving voices to activists banned from the country's public media.

The ruling party Zanu PF, which has been in power for 42 years, faces a serious challenge from newly formed opposition party Citizens Coalition for Change, led by Nelson Chamisa. In the past months, members of the CCC, journalists, trade union leaders, human rights defenders and political activists have been arrested, with most cases still pending before the courts.

But with dissenting voices forced out of mainstream media, social media might offer a new hope. Between 2021 and 2022, the number of social media users in Zimbabwe increased by more than 19% to 1.55 million.

"Twitter has been an amazing networking tool for activists," a human rights and political activist told Index. Out of fear of reprisal from the regime, she asked that her name be changed to Janet. "Because of Twitter, I have met a lot of people and work with them on various issues," she said. "Lots of fundraising has been done using Twitter spaces for political campaigns, for families of activists who have gone missing, for respected figures who have passed away."

But she said that even in the digital world, Zimbabwe remained unsafe for activists like her.

"[We're] dealing with lots of anonymous [social media] accounts, so [you are] never sure who you are really dealing with. Still [there is] an underlying fear which you have to push through. There are those who are called Varakashi, so there is need for vigilance," she said, referring to the army of pro-Mnangagwa social media users who target his critics online.

She hopes that in spite of this threat, social media can be used to track issues that Zimbabweans care about, and put pressure on the regime to change.

The CCC, Janet explained, is a citizens' movement without any official structures.

"This is very frustrating for the ruling party as their tactic has always been to infiltrate and split the opposition from within. We are trying to use TikTok to target the youth, who are apathetic about registering to vote. They feel voting is hopeless," she said.

Richard Mugobo is the founder of The BIG Conversation, a Zimbabwean digital media platform that amplifies issues surrounding open government, transparency and accountability. He said online activists could use social media platforms to raise awareness – debunking fake news, organising events and protests, and verifying statements.

"Politically, platforms such as Twitter, YouTube and WhatsApp could serve the purpose of reaching a broader and diverse audience," he said.

Whatever the opportunities for free expression online, the Zimbabwean government is no stranger to internet shutdowns. In 2019, the digital world went dark amid citizen protests, preventing the spread of information. A similar story unfolded in July 2020, when internet speeds slowed down during protests and people reported being barely able to load tweets.

Social media might offer a platform for dissenting voices, but that platform can just as easily be removed during times of trouble.

The digital world went dark amid citizen protests

Andrew Mambondiyani is a journalist based in Zimbabwe. He has written for publications including BBC and Al Jazeera ✖

51(04):42/45|DOI:10.1177/03064220221144893

CREDIT: Stitchit

Tapestry of tyranny

As political prisoner numbers in Belarus continue to rise, **KATIE DANCEY-DOWNS** speaks to an art collective using traditional embroidery to protest

TWO SWEET FIGURES stand in red thread against fabric, their signature bagpipes slung across their chests and a love heart hovering between connected hands. On first glance, it is a piece of folk embroidery. Symmetrical trees and a repeating border pattern add to the charm. On closer inspection, it is a protest. Immortalised in cross-stitch, the people in the picture are husband and wife Uladzimir and Nadzeya Kalach, the beating hearts of Belarusian fantasy-folk band Irdorath. In December 2021, they were sentenced to two years in a maximum-security prison for "organising and preparing actions that grossly violate public order".

This embroidery is just one of many. Belarusian artist Rufina Bazlova and Moldovan curator Sofia Tocar met in Prague while studying, and formed the Stitchit collective. Their project, Framed in Belarus, immortalises the stories of political prisoners jailed under the regime of President Alexander Lukashenka. Tocar herself stitched the image of Uladzimir Kalach, who is a friend of Bazlova. The real reason they were detained, she said, was that they were filmed playing a song by Soviet rockstar Viktor Tsoi called Khochu Peremen, which is about waiting for

change and has become a popular protest anthem in Belarus.

Following a disputed election and Lukashenka's hold on power, protests broke out in Belarus in 2020. A crackdown ensued and prisons were filled with those involved. Shortly after, Bazlova had the idea of representing political prisoners through art.

"When the protests were in Belarus, it was like something is changing finally, but later it was gone," Bazlova said. "The most important thing left from this fighting for freedom was awareness of political prisoners and how we can see the amount of them [was] still going up. That means the regime is still afraid of the changes that can come."

When they started the project, there were 600 people who Bazlova planned to recreate with cross-stitch. Now, there are thought to be over 1,300 political prisoners in Belarus.

"[Bazlova] realised that she wants to bring attention to each political prisoner, and to make a piece on each of them, but it would not be possible to [do] it by herself. So, the idea came that we need to involve people," Tocar told Index. "It's not only because it logistically makes sense but also because people want to show their solidarity."

This opportunity to show solidarity is the main aim of the duo, and they call it an "artivist" project. People wielding needles and threads in protest come from all around the world. After filling in a web form, they're sent the instructions and designs by the Stitchit team, as well as the story of the person they're going to stitch. If they feel comfortable, they're encouraged to write a letter to the prisoner. Some stitchers have reported back that they received replies to their letters, and so at least some of Lukashenka's prisoners know about the Framed in Belarus project. Viktar Babaryka, a former presidential candidate and key opposition figure sentenced to 14 years in jail, is one of those who is reportedly aware of the project.

"One of the reasons why I decided to realise the project was contact [with] a political prisoner in Belarus," Bazlova explained.

When she initially spoke to Mikhail Yefimovich, she didn't tell him she was planning the project, but he became the first person to feature in an embroidery. Yefimovich was sentenced to two-and-a-half years for violence against a police officer at a protest, which he denies. He's from the same city as Bazlova, and she sent him a letter in prison. Yefimovich replied, in a very touching way.

"It's very important to write letters to them because it's really fresh air. They don't have any news – nothing. The letters are the only important thing that can somehow support them and show they're not forgotten," Bazlova said. Even if a reply doesn't arrive, she said it's important to keep writing and show the regime that people care.

The embroideries are sewn largely in Europe, as well as in the USA, Latin America and China, and in Belarus itself. Both exiles and people still living in the country have taken up their needles and joined the movement. Some embroiderers are interested in the activism while others are drawn in by the craft. While most people create the artwork at home, others join workshops and stitch together, as in the recent Survival Kit 13 art festival in Latvia.

The folk-style patterns, known as ornament, have a history, too. Bazlova explained that when women could not read or write, they created patterns in embroidery to code information. By understanding the language of the patterns, they could read them. Bazlova chose not to use the traditional coded language in her designs to make them more accessible to everyone, but she was inspired to tell the story of Belarus's modern history through traditional Belarusian folk ornament.

For Bazlova, who has made a handful of the embroideries herself and creates the design for every piece, reading more about each political prisoner helps her understand her country better. Learning each story is always painful, but hearing about young prisoners affects her most.

"They're in prison for no reason. Many times, I'm thinking of how their lives will change," Bazlova said. "I have some friends who are still in prison."

The individual embroideries are shown at exhibitions, sometimes with a stitched QR code so people can scan the artwork and find out more about the stories. One recent display was dedicated to Andrei Zeltser, a supporter of the democracy movement who was killed by Belarusian security forces.

"I think political prisoners are actually our future. These are the most brave and the most clever people in Belarus," Bazlova said.

Two more recently sentenced political prisoners rendered in the Framed in Belarus project are former Index staffer Andrei Aliaksandrau and his partner Irina Zlobina, both charged with high treason after paying the fines of protesters. Aliaksandrau was sentenced to 14 years and Zlobina to nine in a closed-door trial.

With rising numbers of prisoners, choosing who to include is a challenge for Stitchit. If the numbers hadn't changed since the start of the project, they would be nearly halfway through.

"It's a dilemma – who is more important and who comes first?" Tocar said. "There is a group of people – politicians, journalists, activists – who are very well known. But then there are workers or people who wrote a comment on the internet and got three years in jail. So, for us, it's also important to speak about these people who don't have much chance to be seen."

Bazlova herself misses her family, but while Lukashenka continues to rule, she cannot risk returning to Belarus.

The final destination for the embroideries is set to be one big quilt – a mosaic of stories that captures this

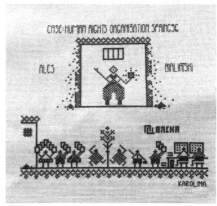

ABOVE: (from top) Mark Bernshtein, a Wikipedia editor sentenced to three years of home arrest, has his story laid out by Stephan Eriksson; as 2022 Nobel Peace Prize winner Ales Bialiatski awaits his trial from prison, his colleague at human rights organisation Spring 96 tells his tale in embroidery

snapshot of Belarusian history. Bazlova and Tocar's dream for this modern-day equivalent of the Bayeux Tapestry is an exhibition in the Museum of Free Belarus. They dream of both the political prisoners and the whole of Belarus being free, so that those depicted in the art can one day see it themselves. ✖

Katie Dancey-Downs is assistant editor at Index

If you want to partipate in the project visit framedinbelarus.net

51(04):46/47|DOI:10.1177/03064220221144894

SPECIAL REPORT

"The archives and the Australian government went to great lengths to oppose my action and to keep the Queen's correspondence secret"

JENNIFER HOCKING | A ROYAL RECKONING | P.59

Crown confidential

The UK Royal Family's obsession with secrecy is blurring history and making it hard for us to get the full picture. An investigation by **MARTIN BRIGHT**

F YOU WANT to understand how deep the UK Royal Family's mania for secrecy runs, just try the following exercise. Go to the website of the National Archives (anyone with a computer and an internet connection can do this) and search the catalogue with the term "Royal Family". It is then possible to filter the search to see which files are "closed" or "retained". Nearly 500 files are categorised in this way, some going back well into the last century, beyond the reign of the late Queen Elizabeth II's father, George VI.

Perhaps not surprisingly, hundreds of these files refer to the short reign of her uncle, Edward VIII, who abdicated in 1936 after less than a year on the throne. Take a closer look and many of these files have absolutely nothing to do with national security, diplomacy or privacy – the usual reasons for withholding government files. In fact, many of them refer to royal memorabilia for Edward's abandoned coronation, which had been due to take place in May 1937. Embarrassing, perhaps, and the Duke of Windsor, as Edward became, remains a controversial figure. But is it really necessary to keep these files sealed for 100 years?

At a stretch, it is possible to imagine the sensitivity of a file about the "Royal Crown and Cypher on pocket watches from Germany", given who was in power in that country at the time, but it's hard to see why files on similar

souvenir items manufactured in Britain such as pens, picture frames, neon signs and wine labels should remain secret 86 years later, let alone closed until 2037.

Other entries are just plain bizarre. A file from 1990-91 is marked closed until 2034. Its title is intriguing: "Petition to the Queen on behalf of Ago Piero Ajano aka HRH Don Juan Alexander Fernando Alphonso of Spain concerning his alleged plight of poverty and ill-treatment in the UK."

It seems Mr Ajano claimed to be the illegitimate son of the Duke of Windsor, and had fallen on hard times. The story is either entirely spurious or utterly sensational: either way, there can be no possible justification for keeping the file secret.

Since 2010, there has been a blanket exemption to the Freedom of Information Act for all official correspondence relating to the monarch, the heir to the throne and the second-in-line to the throne. This was introduced during the decade-long battle by Guardian journalist Rob Evans to gain access to the so-called "black spider memos" from Prince Charles to certain government departments. Evans argued this correspondence constituted lobbying and should be released in the public interest.

"With the black spider memos, Charles was lobbying and trying to influence public policy," Evans told Index. "We ought to know about →

 The idea that all she did was cut a ribbon from time to time is a grotesque misrepresentation

What the royals don't want us to see

FRANCIS CLARKE trawled through hundreds of blocked archives on the UK Royal Family to present a flavour of what is off limits

WATCHING SEASON FIVE of Netflix's lavish Windsor drama, The Crown, my phone was constantly in hand as, eyes flicking from screen to screen, I made cursory Google searches to decipher what was real and what wasn't. Was Boris Yeltsin always drunk? Did Princess Anne eye her future husband through a pair of binoculars? Was Queen Elizabeth II's morning read really The Racing Post?

One episode that really had my fingers typing away was episode five, The Way Ahead. This detailed the events from 1993 when the Sunday Mirror and Sunday People printed recordings of a phone conversation between the then-Prince of Wales and Camilla Parker-Bowles. Intercepted and recorded by an amateur radio enthusiast four years earlier, it arguably damaged Charles' suitability claims as a future king and left Camilla vilified by the press.

No criminal charges were pursued and while it wasn't phone hacking per se, it was clearly an invasion of privacy, a level of which we should all be entitled to. However, as part of this Index investigation, I have been looking through Royal Family records at The National Archives and I can see an abuse of the concept of privacy. Archives that should quite firmly be in the public domain are not.

What's striking is the absurdity, not only of the content but also the length of closure given, of some of the records. For example, a "public record" from 1936 was given access closure for 100 years. This record concerned offensive use of royal emblems in coronation decorations by a company called Dudley and Co Ltd. What could possibly have been so offensive to justify this as a still-closed record? Was a lion on a Royal emblem too cartoonish? With fresh eyes in 2022, we should have the right to see.

There is also an interesting record from 1981 (like the above, it's legal status as a public record) which is the year that Prince Charles married Diana Spencer. We obviously cannot see what's inside. All we know is it's called "News and publicity on the Royal Family". Reconsideration of its blocked status was due in 2019 but there is no note that this happened.

A large number of documents on Edward VIII are blocked. A record from 1985-88 (some of the records only give a timeframe, not a specific year) states: "ROYAL FAMILY. Proposals relating to the papers concerning the abdication of King Edward VIII in 1936". This is information regarding the abdication of a king that happened three years before The Wizard of Oz was released and when Queen Elizabeth II was 10 years old. As it concerns one of the biggest constitutional crises in the nation's history, and one that occurred before most people were born, in whose interest is it to keep this public record closed? Interestingly, it has been retained by the Cabinet Office.

While Freedom of Information requests can be made on most of the records (the option isn't available for the above 1985-88 record, for example), the extreme likelihood is that they will be denied. And believe us, we have tried.

The Royal Family has the right to privacy for things like intimate phone conversations, just like the rest of us. However, the extent of their grip on privacy disallows us access to their public records which, however banal and irrelevant they may be, we should have access to. The question must be asked: If there isn't anything to hide, why are the records still closed?

Francis Clarke is editorial assistant at Index

→ this just as we would if it was a pharmaceutical company."

Evans believes his experience with the memos revealed a wider issue with transparency: "The reality is that the government wraps the royal family

in secrecy in order to protect it from criticism. Whatever you think about the royal family, democracy is degraded because we can't debate this fully if we don't have all the information."

After the death of Elizabeth II on

8 September 2022, two contradictory narratives about her historical legacy came to dominate the instant analysis of her 70-year reign. The first was that she assiduously took a back seat in matters of state and adopted a largely passive constitutional role. The second was that she was instrumental in guiding the country in the post-war period from Empire to Commonwealth. Neither can be entirely true.

Professor Rory Cormac, of the University of Nottingham and co-author of The Secret Royals, says the narrative of non-interference worked powerfully alongside the pageantry associated with the Queen to produce a benign public image of the monarch. But this is a long way from reality.

"She was a political actor and there are consequences. The idea that all she did was cut a ribbon from time to time is a grotesque misrepresentation. They have managed their past incredibly effectively."

Cormac points to three specific areas where more openness would contribute to a greater understanding of the history of the latter half of the 20th century. The first is the Suez Crisis of 1956, just four years into the Queen's reign, when Britain was forced into a humiliating retreat by the USA after initially backing the invasion of Egypt to seize back control of the Suez Canal.

"There is a whole cottage industry on what the Queen knew, and when," said Cormac. "It is a very important case, but historians are just scratching the surface. It's mainly speculation."

The second area is the role played by the monarchy in the end of the empire. Many files in the National Archives referring to royal visits to the former colonies during this period are still closed.

The third, crucially important, subject is Northern Ireland, where the Queen's political role has been largely unexplored by historians. Cormac highlights the example of the royal visit to the province in 1977 – until that point the largest security operation in British history. Files from the government exist, but nothing from the royal side, leaving historians only to speculate.

Cormac and his co-author, Professor Richard Aldrich of Warwick University, are both specialists in the history of intelligence, and the comparison between the royal world and the world of espionage does not go unnoticed in their book:

"Both control and curate their own histories carefully; both are exempt from freedom of information requests. Historians have to wait a long time for intelligence files to make their way to the National Archives – but at least some do eventually arrive. The Royal Family, by contrast, are the real enemies of history. There is no area where restrictions and redactions are so severe."

Cormac is part of a group of historians who believe there needs to be a new approach to royal secrecy. "The argument is that it is a slippery slope," he said. "There is a blanket ban because, they say, where do you draw the line? But this general exemption needs to be challenged."

He and Aldrich have identified a process of historical vandalism carried out by loyal royal flunkeys. Lord Louis Mountbatten and art historian and spy Anthony Blunt went on "raiding parties" across Europe in the post-war period searching for documents on the Windsors. Princess Margaret was notorious for the bonfires she made of her mother's papers. Much else was lost, destroyed or locked away in Windsor Castle.

There is even a file from 1979-80 in the National Archives marked "Royal Family. Duke of Windsor's Papers: allegations by Duc de Grantmesnil that they were stolen by secret agents". It is closed.

In a recent essay entitled Queen Elizabeth and the Commonwealth: Time to Open the Archives, Philip Murphy, director of history and policy at the Institute of Historical Research, said: "Its obsessive secrecy combined with the length of the reign of Queen Elizabeth

There is no evidence that King Charles has a more open attitude to royal history than his mother did

II means we probably have no more accurate a sense of how the monarchy has operated in our lifetimes than our grandparents and great-grandparents did in theirs."

As Murphy and others point out, the reach of vetting teams from the Cabinet Office who have charge of what should and shouldn't be published spreads way beyond the National Archives themselves. The personal archives of past prime ministers (Anthony Eden at the University of Birmingham and Harold Macmillan in Oxford) are subject to restrictions on royal material.

Meanwhile, the royal archives at Windsor give no access whatsoever to files on the reign of Elizabeth II, which include correspondence not just with prime ministers of the UK but premiers and governors-general of the Commonwealth realms. Even historians wishing to gain access to files from previous reigns are obliged to sign a form to say they will inform Buckingham Palace how any material will be used. Cameras are forbidden.

There are also files which have been reclassified after historians found information that proved uncomfortable to the Royal Family. A Metropolitan Police file (MEPO 10/35) on the protection arrangements for the Prince of Wales from 1935 showed that his security detail was spying on the future king and his lover Wallis Simpson. Details of Simpson's affair with a married man, Guy Trundle, are laid out in salacious detail. A note on the affair to the Metropolitan Police commissioner marked "secret" was first released in 2003 and details of the file's contents featured in Portillo's State Secrets, a BBC series on the National Archives fronted by the former politician Michael

Portillo. Yet any historian attempting to access MEPO 10/35 today will find it is "closed whilst access is under review". No further explanation is given.

Murphy told Index: "The Palace has an instinct to micromanage and use deference." In this case, this instinct seems particularly petty-minded as the information is already in the public domain. Most historians interested in the period will already have electronic versions of the file. The note on Simpson's affair with Trundle is published in all its juicy detail on the website of the National Archives. Portillo's programme is available to anyone with access to YouTube.

In some cases, the royal fetish for secrecy has left serious gaps in the historical record. For instance, why is so little of detail known about Prince George, Duke of Kent, the youngest brother of Edward VIII and George VI? He was a fascinating and controversial figure – a bisexual playboy who is alleged to have had affairs with film stars and celebrities from the jazz age including Noel Coward. In 1942, George died in an air crash in Scotland while serving in the RAF. He was the only member of the Royal Family for many centuries to have died on active duty. The notes from the Court of Inquiry into the incident were immediately lost and the circumstances of the crash remain shrouded in mystery. The incident is significant because there have been suggestions that the prince flouted wartime regulations to carry out the mission.

In the early 2000s, a veteran royal writer began a project to write George's biography, but his mission was immediately hampered by the lack of information in the official record. He →

PICTURED:
The marriage of
Edward VIII to
Wallis Simpson in
France following his
abdication from the
British throne, June
1937. Many files on
Edward are blocked
from public access
indefinitely

The Royal Family ruthlessly seek to rewrite history to their own advantage

→ told Index: "I first visited the National Archives at Kew but Kent's file, when I ordered it up, had quite obviously been weeded." The author wrote to the Royal Archives in Windsor only to be informed that there were many calls on the time of the keepers of the records and that on this occasion they would be unable to oblige. He has since given up on the idea of writing the biography and the full life story of Prince George remains untold.

"A family which relies on public support to retain its primacy in British social life has, I believe, a duty to act responsibly when it comes to breaking the law, especially during wartime," he said. "The actions of the Royal Archives in disallowing me access to Kent's files (which in any case, it's my certain belief, would have been severely edited) amounts to censorship, nothing more or less."

In order to maintain good relations with Buckingham Palace, the author does not wish to be named here, but he remains furious at the lack of openness: "My belief is that everyone is entitled to a certain measure of privacy, but there can be no question that the Royal Family, and those who surround them, ruthlessly seek to rewrite history to their own advantage."

The writer cites an extraordinary example from the time of the abdication crisis. In government papers from the time, he discovered considerable concern that "Bertie" (the future George VI) was not up to the job of taking over from Edward VIII. Instead, the idea was floated that Queen Mary should become Regent while the dust settled, and the crown would then pass to Prince George. Had this happened, the present Duke of Kent would now be King and not Charles III.

"How the Royal Family manages their affairs in such circumstances is of great importance to historians and, it can be argued, to the nation," the writer added. "But without access to the Palace papers no accurate record of this event has been written and it's altogether been bypassed by historians."

As part of Index's investigation into royal secrecy, we sent a survey to two dozen journalists and historians who specialise in the area. Of those who responded, all but one said their research had been affected by the refusal of the archives to grant access to key materials.

A handful of historians have chosen to fight back. Most prominent of these is Andrew Lownie, the biographer of Edward and Mrs Simpson and the Mountbattens (see article on p.57). For four years, at great personal expense, Lownie has been pushing for the release of the diaries and personal correspondence of Lord Louis Mountbatten, the late Prince Philip's uncle and mentor to the present king. While these were bought by the University of Southampton using £4.5 million of public money, full public access was blocked at every stage – first by the university and then by an exceptional ministerial directive from the Cabinet Office. Following intervention from the Information Commissioner's Office, the files were finally released earlier this year, but costs were not awarded to Lownie, who spent more than £300,000 of his own money on the case. It was, in short, only a half victory and a battle that should never have been fought to start with.

In a more clear-cut victory, Professor Jenny Hocking, of Monash University in Melbourne, successfully challenged the National Archives of Australia to release correspondence between the Queen and the Australian Governor-General, Sir John Kerr, from 1975 (see article on p.59). In that year Kerr dismissed →

Royal secrecy surveyed

As part of our special report Index sent a survey to 28 historians and journalists who work with archives related to the Royal Family. We received 10 responses. The majority wanted to remain anonymous – interesting in and of itself. Below we highlight some of the trends and comments

EIGHT OUT OF 10 respondents said they had been unable to conduct their work researching the royal family without conflict, difficulty or compromise beyond that encountered in other areas of their research. One believed it has become worse. They said: "As a journalist visiting the National Archives I have noticed that in recent years almost all government files relating to royalty have been withheld long beyond what would have been the previous 30 year limit. Increasing deference?"

In answer to the question "Have you ever tried to access information that should be publicly available related to the royal family (including their close friends and associates) but is not" only one answered no. Please note this person was also happy to be named – the historian Andrew Roberts – and was keen to highlight he has never had a bad experience researching the royals, a fact that should go on the record here. In contrast to Roberts' positive experience, another historian had a glut of negative ones, ranging from "false statements made by government departments and other public authorities and retention of files by government departments under blanket 'Lord Chancellor instruments' for decades (abusing a proviso in the Public Records Act) instead of transferring them to the National Archives" to the "chaotic state of the Metropolitan Police's archives, including 'missing' files" and "the 'sealing' of royal wills".

Six told us they had looked for material in the archive related to the royal family and found it had been removed. Needless to say they all found that suspicious. On this one comment is worth noting: 'I was told when working at the Lambeth Palace Library Archives that some sources held by the library relating to the Royal Family for the 1940s and 1950s were simply not available for researchers to consult, as per the request of the Royal Archives. Whilst engaged with the BBC Written Archives, their policy on royal material was also updated (as per a request of the royal liaison) which meant that any previously unseen BBC files relating to royalty had to be vetted and sensitive information removed before it could be presented to researchers."

Given the prevalence of SLAPPs in the UK – strategic lawsuits against public participation – we were curious about whether there were any members of the royal family that people would not write about negatively for fear of legal or reputational repercussions. The answer here was mixed. Three said yes but the rest said no.

All except two believed that access to the Royal Archives should be covered by freedom of information legislation. Most comments for yes were similar to this: "Because the monarchy is a public institution. I believe the Royal Archives' current opt out of FoI requests is based on the royal family being a 'private' family. This has clearly not been the case for more than 150 years: the monarchy is a public institution of state. And, as an institution of state, the monarchy needs to be accountable."

Interestingly five said the Keeper of the Queen's (now King's) Archive does not act in a transparent way in terms of granting access to the Royal Archives. One provided more context: "They seem to operate according to a pre-determined list of documents that are regarded as off-limits - even to the point of going to court to ensure that Prince Philip's will should be embargoed for 90 years."

Finally, the real crunch question - we asked whether anyone had ever wanted to publish something on the Royal Family and not been able to. This was a 50-50 split.

→ the Labor prime minister Gough Whitlam following a constitutional crisis in which the opposition blocked government business by its control of the upper house of parliament, the Senate. The publication of Hocking's The Palace Letters show the Queen was in regular correspondence with the governor-general about the possibility of Gough's dismissal for several weeks. They present a picture of political engagement by the monarch which is very different from the approach the Palace prefers to project.

The work of Lownie and Hocking demonstrates that it is possible to push back against the official wall of silence. But it also shows the lengths to which the establishment is prepared to go to maintain royal secrecy. The Australian National Archives spent $1.7 million of public money contesting the release of the "Palace Letters" and it is not known how much the UK government spent fighting the Mountbatten release – but it is likely to be a similar sum.

There is no evidence that King Charles has a more open attitude to royal history than his mother did. Indeed, he has every reason to keep the papers from the Queen's reign that refer to his own indiscretions securely locked away in Windsor Castle.

However, despite official efforts, the edifice of secrecy is crumbling. As historians of the Commonwealth further investigate the UK's colonial past, it is unlikely the Palace will be able to maintain its tight control of the historical narrative in the way it has done in the UK itself. As Philip Murphy has written: "This sort of push-back against the Royal Family's obsession with secrecy is more likely to be effective outside the UK than in Britain itself, where the Palace still exerts considerable influence over a distinctly deferential political class."

The legacy of imperialism is the Achilles heel of royal secrecy. It will become increasingly difficult for the Palace to maintain the narrative about the role of the Queen in the successful transition from Empire to Commonwealth without allowing access to the documentary evidence to prove it. ✖

Martin Bright is editor-at-large at Index

Visit our website for more on our campaign #EndRoyalSecrecacy

51(04):50/56|DOI:10.1177/03064220221144907

Secrets, lies and a costly legal battle

The historian **ANDREW LOWNIE** has paid dearly in his quest to access archives on Mountbatten, which should have been readily available. Here he writes about the personal toll

ABOVE: Queen Elizabeth II and Lord Mountbatten

NO PRIVATE INDIVIDUAL should be financially ruined seeking access to material, which was purchased with taxpayers' money on the basis that it would be open to the public. But that is the position in which I now find myself.

As a biographer, I rely on historical documents to recreate the past and some of the most useful sources are private diaries and letters, as they are generally written in the immediacy of the moment and reflect the most intimate feelings of the writers. So when in 2015 I embarked on a joint biography of the last Viceroy of India and his wife, Dickie and Edwina Mountbatten, I looked forward to consulting their extensive diaries and correspondence, which had already been quoted in various books on them.

I was surprised when the archivists at the University of Southampton, where the Mountbatten's papers are held, claimed to know nothing about them. →

→ This, in spite of Southampton leading a huge fundraising campaign to buy them in 2011 for £2.8 million - made up of a grant of £2 million from the National Heritage Memorial Fund, £100,000 from Hampshire County Council and £1.6m in lieu of taxes. The press releases, after completion of the sale, stressed they would "be freely available to all".

After I pressed them, Southampton then claimed that under the Acceptance in Lieu (AIL) arrangements with HMRC, it was bound by a 'Ministerial Direction' of 5 August 2011 from complying with requests for access to any information contained in the diaries or letters. The genesis of this seemingly unique 'Ministerial Direction' remains mysterious, as neither the university nor the Cabinet Office will even identify the signatory. Indeed, under FOI requests, no government department has accepted any responsibility for it.

Over the next few years I was repeatedly forced to call on the intervention of the Information Commissioner's Office to force the Cabinet Office and Southampton to respond properly to my FOI requests to discover what had happened to the diaries and letters. In April 2019 the Information Commissioner's Office served contempt proceedings against the university in the High Court, a step unprecedented against a public authority. And, in December 2019, it issued a Decision Notice ruling that the diaries and letters should be released, a decision which the Cabinet Office and Southampton appealed, even though they knew from a review the previous year that the material was completely innocuous.

Just before the four-day hearing in November 2021, Southampton abandoned their reliance on the 'Ministerial Direction'. On such grounds, the Cabinet Office had no role to play in the hearing, no right to 'review' anything or to dictate to Southampton what to do re the Freedom

CREDIT: Fox Photos/Stringer

Their strategy appears to have been one of obfuscation and delay

of Information Act, but this was ignored by the tribunal.

The appeal had also become academic because pre-hearing 99% of the material, some 30,000 pages, had been released, though the tribunal did rule that the Cabinet Office still had the right to apply FOIA exemptions to the diaries and letters which meant that just over a hundred redactions – some a single word, others several paragraphs – were applied on the grounds they were communications with the Sovereign, and that they would damage international relations or national security.

Even though I had succeeded in securing the release of most of the material, my application for costs was dismissed, leaving me with a legal bill of almost £500,000. From the outset the University and Cabinet Office deployed extensive teams of lawyers, including two top barristers, all at taxpayers' expense, and their strategy appears to have been one of obfuscation and delay at every stage and to break me financially. Their bill must have been at least double mine but even after Parliamentary Questions and media enquiries, they will not reveal it. Interestingly the Cabinet Office seems to have picked up most of Southampton's legal bills.

One has to ask why an academic institution, presumably in favour of scholarship being made available and in academic freedom, is censoring private diaries and letters ostensibly on behalf of the government, for which there is no legal justification in what seems an unquestioning relationship between a public research institution and the State.

Many questions remain. Why are the Cabinet Office paying most of Southampton's costs? Why hasn't the option to release the Nehru-Edwina correspondence, bought under the same agreement, been exercised, as it could have been at any time for £100 since 2016?

My fight to secure rightful public access to the diaries and letters, which if sold to almost any other academic institution, would have been available over a decade ago, has come at both a heavy financial cost – monies earmarked for my retirement and to pass on to my children – and some ostracisation from fellow historians who clearly have no wish to upset the establishment. My biography, The Mountbattens, published in 2019, though a bestseller would also have been richer and more nuanced.

My faith in the integrity of the Civil Service and judicial system has been shattered. Repeatedly I saw government ministers lie to Parliament, the media and even to my lawyers – when they could be bothered to respond at all. Dr David Owen, who took up my case, was dismissed by a senior Cabinet official with numerous untruths. Letters to the vice chancellor and the supposedly independent Council of the University of Southampton went unanswered.

But I continue to try and work within the FOI system, though it needs reform and proper regulatory powers, to tell the story of the past as accurately as I can. I feel it has been worthwhile to fight to make available an important historical archive and also to make a stand for access to archives, the need for trust and transparency in public institutions and against censorship and the abuse of power, many of the issues on which Index on Censorship has so effectively campaigned for so many years. ✖

Andrew Lownie is a British biographer

51(04):57/58|DOI:10.1177/03064220221144908

LEFT: Elizabeth II and Prince Philip meet then-Governor-General of Australia, John Kerr, in 1977

A royal reckoning

Queen Elizabeth II played a central role in the dismissal of an Australian prime minister – a move that was kept hidden for 45 years. Historian **JENNIFER HOCKING** went to court to reveal this secret, and here she discusses her battle

AT THE HEART of the carefully constructed public image of the modern monarchy in the UK is the longstanding presumption of "royal secrecy". Secrecy and its correlating control of the historical record is the monarchy's great protector in an age of rising democratic expectations of transparency and accountability, and the bane of historians across the Commonwealth.

The routine denial of public access to archives and public records containing any royal reference, even centuries old, without royal approval is hardwired into every archival holding under the spurious label of "personal". The Royal Family draws on its private/public duality – as both a family and a constitutional entity – to keep politically-compromising documents secret by claiming they're personal and not part of its constitutional role. This dynastic power to suppress vests the monarchy with a unique capacity to craft its own narrative and to control its history – our shared history.

The pervasive reach of royal secrecy, however, reflects a deeper issue – its impact on the historical record. Faced with the impossible task of writing history when a key constitutional element has been excised from it, we construct a distorted and incomplete one in which the Royal Family appears, if at all, purely on its own terms. The essential "political neutrality of the Crown" required of a constitutional monarchy (which Buckingham Palace claims is always adhered to) is a sophistry enabled and perpetuated by secrecy.

Australian history furnishes us with a particularly egregious example of royal intervention in political matters and its subsequent denial. This was the dismissal without warning of the Gough Whitlam Labor government in 1975 by the governor-general, Sir John Kerr. The Queen's private secretary, Sir Martin Charteris, immediately and emphatically denied that the Queen played any part in this dramatic rupture with constitutional practice, and history was written accordingly.

My research into Kerr's papers in the National Archives of Australia as I worked on Whitlam's biography quickly told me otherwise. The Queen was very much involved in the dismissal. Kerr's reference to "Sir Martin Charteris's advice to me on dismissal" was just one example. An immense trove of more than 200 secret letters between the Queen and Kerr had been in the archives for decades, their release embargoed by the Queen. Although the Archives Act (Aust) requires the release of official records after 20 years, the archives claimed the letters were "personal" and refused to release them.

And so, when I was presented with the unexpected opportunity to secure access to these extraordinarily significant "Palace letters" and challenge royal secrecy, I took it. →

Australian history furnishes us with a particularly egregious example of royal intervention in political matters and its subsequent denial

The archives and the Australian government went to great lengths to oppose my action and to keep the Queen's correspondence secret

→ It is now 50 years since the election of Whitlam's reformist Labor government. After 23 years of Conservative rule, Whitlam came to office with an ambitious agenda for reform grounded in equality of opportunity through enhanced education and health provision, electoral reform, a commitment to human rights, women's rights, racial equality and Indigenous land rights, an independent foreign policy and the end of "relics of colonialism" in Australia's relations with the UK.

Yet, just three years later, and after a second election victory in May 1974, Whitlam was sensationally dismissed by the governor-general on 11 November 1975 with an unprecedented use of the "reserve powers of the Crown". This exercise of an arcane royal prerogative to dismiss an elected government was "one of the most controversial and tumultuous events in the modern history of the nation" according to the Federal Court.

Inevitably, the use of the reserve powers by the governor-general, the Queen's representative in Australia, raised questions about her possible involvement in Whitlam's dismissal – an involvement which has always been denied. As the Queen's then deputy private secretary Sir William Heseltine

later described it: "The Palace was in a state of total ignorance." This, we now know, was completely untrue.

In 2016, I started action in the Federal Court against the archives, seeking public access to the Palace letters. An exceptional team of lawyers all working on a pro bono basis made this challenge possible: Antony Whitlam QC, Bret Walker SC and Tom Brennan SC, instructed by Corrs Chambers Westgarth. The costs of legal remedy are disarmingly prohibitive, and funding this case was a constant concern during the four-year legal battle.

Buckingham Palace was closely involved from the outset and argued vehemently against the release of the letters. The Queen's private secretary claimed that their continued secrecy was essential "to preserve the constitutional position of the monarch and the monarchy".

The archives and the Australian government went to great lengths to oppose my action and to keep the Queen's correspondence secret. Australia's second law officer, the Commonwealth solicitor-general, Stephen Donaghue QC, led the archives' legal team and when the case reached the High Court of Australia in 2020, the first law officer, attorney-general Christian Porter, joined with the archives in contesting my claim. It was obvious and daunting institutional pressure from the highest level of government.

In May 2020, after two devastating defeats in the lower courts, the High Court of Australia ruled in my favour in an emphatic 6:1 decision. The court found that the Palace letters were not "personal" and that they were subject to the public access provisions of the Archives Act, overturning the Queen's embargo over their release.

It was a stark rejection of the claim by the archives and Buckingham Palace.

"We cannot see how the correspondence could appropriately be described, however 'loosely', as 'private or personal records'," the judges wrote.

CREDIT: Keystone Press/Alamy

The Palace letters cast a rare light on the way in which royal secrecy operates on archival holdings and the disappointing compliance of the National Archives of Australia in maintaining royal secrecy. We faced the humiliating spectacle of the nation's foremost archival repository, tasked with maintaining and facilitating access to its most significant historical records, arguing against its ownership and control of this historic royal correspondence.

The NAA's decision to contest my case was immensely costly for it – reputationally and financially. The High Court ordered it to pay my entire legal costs from the Federal Court to the High Court. In the end the archives spent more than Aus $1.7m in unsuccessfully contesting the case in its efforts to keep its own historical records secret. It was completely antithetical to the core

ABOVE: Pro-Whitlam demonstrators walking through the streets of Sydney after the sacking of Prime Minister Gough Whitlam on 11 November 1975

functions of our national archives, for which it was roundly condemned.

The archives finally released the Queen's correspondence with the governor-general in full on 14 July 2020. It was a great victory for our history and for transparency, and it has transformed the history of Whitlam's dismissal.

The letters put beyond question that the Queen and the then Prince Charles were involved in the governor-general's decision to dismiss the government. Charles fully supported Kerr's actions and, like his uncle and mentor Lord Louis Mountbatten, wrote to Kerr soon after the dismissal to tell him so. "What you did ... was right and the courageous thing to do," he told him.

The letters have finally revealed what Buckingham Palace always denied

– that the Queen was involved in Kerr's decision to dismiss the government, and kept that involvement secret from Whitlam. The Queen and Charles's discussions with Kerr about the move began in September 1975, two months before the dismissal. The letters show that they advised the governor-general on the existence and use of the "reserve power" to remove the government, at times encouraging him to do so. It is a shocking revelation which should have been known to the prime minister at the time and to the Australian people since.

The repeated denials by Buckingham Palace that the Queen played any part in the dismissal were simply untrue, as these letters have now shown. Through her private secretary, the Queen advised Kerr on his power to dismiss, on

whether Whitlam could seek his recall from office, and what her response to that key question would be.

And in her final letter before the dismissal, she told Kerr that the use of the reserve powers against the government, "cannot possibly do the monarchy any avoidable harm. The chances are you will do it good".

Within hours of the letters' release in 2020, Buckingham Palace issued a rare public statement asserting that they confirmed that "neither Her Majesty nor the Royal Household had any part to play in Kerr's decision to dismiss Whitlam".

This perverse position is impossible to reconcile with the history as we now know it from the Queen's own letters.

The continued denial by the palace of this now incontrovertible fact only prolongs its political intervention – this time in the history of that divisive episode, a constitutional aberration in which the Queen and Prince Charles should never have been involved.

Royal secrecy is a powerful and pervasive form of censorship, denying historians access to key documents that would reveal the monarch's political involvements, extending even to intervention in the written history.

Letters between Kerr and Buckingham Palace after the dismissal show that the Queen's private secretary also vetted Kerr's autobiography prior to its publication to hide this involvement. While claiming to present the "facts" and "truth" about the dismissal, Kerr's selective memoir did no such thing.

This direct intervention of Buckingham Palace in the written history constructed a royally vetted version of the dismissal – one in which the Queen was not involved. This flawed history would still be in place today had my legal action not succeeded. ✖

Jennifer Hocking is an historian and the award-winning author of The Palace Letters

51(04):59/61|DOI:10.1177/03064220221144909

Never get your face stuck in the wrong book again
Special introductory offer for new subscribers...

Your first issue free!

Strong Words is the literary magazine that helps
you pick your next book with confidence
and accuracy, and makes reading about what's new
feel a pleasure in itself – never like homework.
£45 for a year's six issues + the latest issue FREE

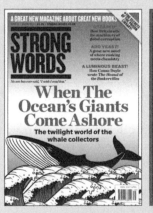 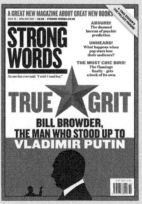   

Or spread the cost by paying £22.50 every six months, or £3.75 a month.
Whatever your taste in books, there'll always be something to meet your needs,
and plenty more you didn't know you needed besides.

Subscribe using code INDEX23 at:
www.webscribe.co.uk/magazine/strongwords
Or call now on: 01442 820580

It's time to start reading like never before

COMMENT

"The explanation for the bill on the Home Office website makes it sound benign – it is anything but"

DANNY SHAW | UK LAW RISKS CRIMINALISING THE INNOCENT | P.70

Down with a disclaimer

Those who argue Netflix's The Crown should have a fictional disclaimer not only misunderstand art, they meddle with it, argues **MARC NASH**

AN EX-PRIME MINISTER and a dame of British film and theatre have both criticised the latest series of the Netflix drama The Crown about the British Royal Family. Sir John Major criticised a plot line in which he featured, saying the depicted events never happened. Dame Judi Dench renewed calls for the producers to include a disclaimer with each episode. "No one is a greater believer in artistic freedom than I, but this cannot go unchallenged," she said. Passing over her qualifying her free expression credentials, which rather serves to undermine both these credentials and the force of what she is going on to state, all involved seem to fail to understand the nature of art. Even the producers have labelled their artistic endeavour "fictionalised drama" which is a tautology. The clue lies in the word 'drama' – that alone renders it fiction. When you add actors, script and performance into the mix, it only further solidifies the fictive nature of the work.

> The clue lies in the word 'drama' – that alone renders it fiction

No disclaimer is required.

Recently crowned Nobel laureate for literature Annie Ernaux writes fiction. Fiction based on her own life and experiences. Her work has been labelled "autofiction". Ernaux herself shot this label down in an interview at Barnard College in the USA, arguing that she never approaches her work with the critical term of autofiction in mind, nor does she desire to fictionalise herself and her life. (Her UK publishers Fitzcarraldo Editions have her work in their non-fiction imprint, yet handily she was nominated for the 2019 Booker International Prize, which is a prize solely for translated fiction. For Ernaux, what makes it fiction is its narrative form. This is crucial in understanding that any narrative art form is rendered fictional by the very act of organising its material into a narrative. It employs artifice, for purposes of comprehensibility and perhaps also to deliver a set of meanings to its audience. The supposed factual forms of memoir and (auto-)biography inevitably both employ a narrative to drive readers through the pages so that they build up a picture of the subject. Yet they overlook that the sequences of events depicted are artfully arranged for these reasons, rather than necessarily sticking

ABOVE: John Major and Queen Elizabeth II

to the exact way in which they unfolded. Simultaneity is always a problem in narrative as to how to reproduce it. More often than not, the events are separated out rather than superimposed temporally in a narrative. And this does not account for the subjectivity of the writer in considering their subject (even when the subject is themselves).

All narrative art therefore embodies fictional elements. Even the genre distinctions between fiction and non-fiction becomes questionable. Where non-fiction pursues more academic pursuits such as history, or science, there is a question as to whether such literature even rates as art at all. Genre and labelling is reductive, trying to squeeze any artwork into pre-defined categories. It's diminishing towards the art, the artist and the audience alike, as it presumes to direct their freedom of interpretation. Dame Judi is calling for a labelling, when in truth we are not fully in control of what artistic labels mean. Just ask a Nobel laureate. ✖

Marc Nash is a London-based novelist

51(04):64/64|DOI:10.1177/03064220221144910

'The Satanic Verses is the rude contrary of the authoritarian lie'

HANIF KUREISHI's powerful tribute to Salman Rushdie about the author's fantastic alternative to one-dimensional, corrosive fascism

ABOVE: Salman Rushdie holds The Satanic Verses, 1988

FRIENDS AND ASSOCIATES of Salman Rushdie gathered at London's British Library back in October to celebrate the Booker winner's work. Rushdie, who is a firm advocate of free expression and contributor to this magazine, lived under threat for decades after Iran's Ayatollah Khomeini issued a *fatwa* over his novel The Satanic Verses in 1989. His stabbing in August while on stage in Upstate New York was a shocking reminder that the voices of hate remain. The suspect had reportedly read only two pages of the book. In an act of solidarity, passages from his large collection of writings were read out at the event, alongside various other speeches and recollections. Index has the privilege of publishing Hanif Kureishi's powerful tribute, printed for the first time here with permission. ✖

51(04):65/65|DOI:10.1177/03064220221144912

The Spectre

Hanif Kureishi

THERE IS A spectre always haunting the world. Sometimes it is further away, other times it is close. But it is always present, always a possibility, and always has to be fought.

This spectre is the political and religious idea called fascism. This contamination is, as we know, common in the world, and becoming ever closer and more common, leaving the liberalism and democracy we like to take for granted in its wake.

And fascism, like literature, is personal as well as political; it is inside the human being, as well as outside, as ideology. It can, as we know, become a state of mind, even of our own minds, of course.

And what a mind it is that fascism creates. An arid, one-dimensional place, a terror state stuck in the past, where there cannot be any complexity or doubt, and which separates the internal population into 'us' and 'them'. Nothing new can be taken in. It claims to know everything already. It is a simplified, purged, antiseptic and childish idea of the world which requires the annihilation of all opposition, as well as, in its public dimension, the destruction of journalism, universities, and free thought.

If fascism is all noisy slogans, flags, propaganda and the idealisation of fatuous leaders; if fascism is a dehumanising patriarchal monologue that never ends, The Satanic Verses is the rude contrary of the authoritarian lie. It is resistance to God, who is the ultimate fascist, along with his sycophants, because the novel is, in itself, a debate, a conversation, an argument worth having. The Satanic Verses is a rollicking, whirling, kaleidoscopic book of upsidedownness, and of through-the-looking-glass-ness. It is rich with jokes, wit, dreams, reversals and questions. It is as real and difficult and complex as the world, as it celebrates the importance, necessity and beauty of blasphemy.

In a way, you could say that it is freewheeling literary madness that keeps us sane in this 'out of joint' time, and that literature, made from the alchemy of reason and the imagination, reminds us that there always is an alternative, that we can be creative, that we are not at the end, that we can make new things, bringing, as Rushdie puts it, 'newness into the world'.

In the face of the horror and sadness of what has occurred, we should recall that The Satanic Verses is an essential book, an always urgent and crucial novel which prompts us not to forget that our colleague and friend, Salman Rushdie, has devoted his life to struggling with the spectre of authoritarianism on our behalf.

He has taken responsibility as we all must. And we give him thanks here today, for his bravery and heroism. We wish him well in his recovery. Thank you, Salman, for what you have given us.

Hanif Kureishi is a British award-winning playwright, screenwriter, filmmaker and novelist

Jamaica needs to be a republic – now

Leaving the Commonwealth isn't just a matter of preference, it's a matter of freedom, writes **ROSALEA HAMILTON**

IN THE WAKE of Queen Elizabeth II's death, Jamaicans became more aware of the absurdity of having a foreign monarch as head of state. The official 12 days of mourning and the imposition of King Charles III as the new head sparked further debates about the relevance of Jamaica's constitutional monarchy. More than ever before, the costs and benefits were open to scrutiny.

The voice of republican advocacy had grown louder when the Duke and Duchess of Cambridge (now the Prince and Princess of Wales) visited Jamaica in March 2022. In the context of the Covid-19 pandemic and its economic impact, many were concerned about bread-and-butter issues and viewed government spending on the royal visit as misplaced.

Among them were parents who had lost their jobs or their businesses and consequently struggled to send their children back to school. One young mother expressed the view of many: "If a republic will improve how I live, I'm all for it."

|||| The Jamaican people must believe in themselves as sovereign owners of their country

Republican values of liberty, freedom and inalienable human rights have had a long history in Jamaica, dating back to 1494 when Indigenous people faced genocide with the arrival of Christopher Columbus. From the mid-1600s, British imperial domination meant people suffered the atrocities and inhumanity of slavery and colonisation. Centuries of resistance followed.

Even after emancipation in 1838, when the system of slavery was abolished there, the dream of freedom quickly became a nightmare. The institutional legacies of slavery persisted, fostering decades of resistance. With independence in 1962 came the promise of self-government. But so, too, came constitutional provisions which deeply entrenched the monarch as head of state, giving centralised executive powers, largely exercised by the cabinet under the control of the prime minister.

Jamaica's constitutional monarchy persists 60 years later. The centuries-old dreams of freedom and the aspirations for self-determination remain unfulfilled. But a new era might be on the horizon.

After Barbados became a republic in November 2021, the republican debate was reignited in Jamaica. There has been no move to establish a republic since 1995, when the Joint Select Committee on Constitutional and Electoral Reform had agreed, among other things, to create a republic by removing the monarch as head of state. They also agreed to "Jamaicanising" the constitution, making it a "product of the Jamaican people".

Since then, despite commitments by

ABOVE: Prince William visits a teachers' college in Jamaica as part of the Platinum Jubilee Royal Tour of the Caribbean, March 2022

the country's two main political parties to end the constitutional monarchy, the old political order has remained intact. Neither political party has brought in adequate mechanisms for the Jamaican people to influence policy. Instead, expressions of discontent filtered into music and popular culture, accompanied

The centuries-old dreams of freedom and the aspirations for self-determination remain unfulfilled

by demands for change from civil society advocacy. These demands have been largely ignored or inadequately addressed. Today, Jamaica's 1962 independence constitution remains as a British "Order in Council" and not a product of the Jamaican people.

It's also possible that Jamaicans have so far lacked the self-confidence to do anything. In 2012, 40% of Jamaicans supported the monarchy, but things are changing. A poll in July 2022 revealed that only 27% supported the monarchy, with 56% in favour of Jamaica stepping away from the crown.

If we want a Jamaican republic, there are two key issues we must address. First, we need mechanisms that enable politicians to hear the voice of the people. This is essential not only in addressing the will of the people but also in unleashing Jamaica's creative potential and enhancing competitiveness. We need to embrace opportunities such as participatory budgeting, which allows creative entrepreneurs to champion their ideas for financing products that are innovative and can compete globally.

Next, we must replace the monarch as Jamaica's head of state. We need a local leader who signs laws on behalf of the people and exercises additional powers defined by the people.

For any meaningful change, the Jamaican people must believe in themselves as sovereign owners of their country and they need to be willing to undertake the responsibility of self-government. Republicanism must lead to improved institutions – ones that empower people to address the issues of today and improve living standards. If we have this, communities can be involved in local decision-making and deal with persistent inter-generational problems. Criminality, landlessness and poverty can then be properly addressed.

To get to that point, it's vital we have effective public education that deepens the understanding of republicanism in Jamaica as part of our long road to freedom. The Jamaican people must speak up and, most importantly, be heard. ✖

Rosalea Hamilton is the founding director of the Institute of Law and Economics in Kingston, Jamaica. She is part of The Advocates Network, which is a non-partisan alliance of individuals and organisations advocating for human rights and good governance in Jamaica

51(04):66/67|DOI:10.1177/03064220221144913

Report first, talk later...

Our media is increasingly governed by the desire to be noticed rather than be accurate, and all the poorer for it argues **RICHARD SAMBROOK**

WE ARE DROWNING in opinion. From TV panel shows masquerading as news, to deliberately provocative talk radio, to newspaper columnists seeking attention to social media argument eliding into abuse. Some of it, of course, offers insight and expands perspectives. Much of it entertains. But too little of it informs or educates – those other pillars of public service media which seek to strengthen democracy and expand the public space. Too much of today's media is focused on generating profitable heat rather than more complex light. It's an attention economy where being noticed rather than being right breeds success.

How did we get here? Largely through the incentives of a highly competitive commercial digital media. First the explosion of cable and satellite TV in the 1980s. The loosening of regulation with the scrapping of the Fairness Doctrine in 1987 allowed a new raft of largely right-wing, highly opinionated talk radio and then TV to profitably emerge. For them, talk was cheap and easy but reporting was expensive and hard. Other countries followed suit.

The UK still has broadcast regulation to deliver political impartiality, but the regulator Ofcom has relaxed its position in support of allowing greater freedom of speech. So for example, LBC radio has successfully met its regulatory requirement for impartiality by offering

ABOVE: BBC news reporter Emily Maitlis interviews a member of Extinction Rebellion. Maitlis recently accused the BBC of "both-sidesism"

a range of highly opinionated shows from across the political spectrum; new TV services followed with presenters like Nigel Farage, Dan Wootton or Mark Steyn on GB News or Piers "I'm an opinion machine" Morgan on TalkTV.

Increased competition has led to shriller broadcasting in the hope of attention. This has been exacerbated by the internet and social media where clicks mean profit. Clips from low audience TV shows can get millions of online views, and greater revenue, if the headline presses the right emotional buttons.

In turn we have seen the rise of journalists as celebrities commanding

big salaries and their own fanbase. The recent departure of some of the BBC's biggest names to talk radio and podcasting offers them a higher personal profile and salary. The BBC's former political editor Andrew Marr said he was looking forward to "getting his voice back" as he left for his own LBC talk show – although in truth he says little such a skilled broadcaster couldn't say at the BBC.

These programmes feed off the polarised politics of the moment – what one commentator has called the "footballification of politics" where it doesn't matter if your side is right or wrong: what matters is tribal loyalty. And we have the rise of identity politics and advocacy, particularly online, stirring deep emotions and

CREDIT: Penelope Barritt/Alamy

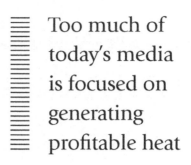

Too much of today's media is focused on generating profitable heat

non-negotiable positions of principle.

In this colourful, noisy, disputatious environment – with a mushrooming of perspectives and a host of new digital formats – a commitment to facts and evidence can appear fusty and is frequently misunderstood.

The BBC's former Newsnight presenter Emily Maitlis left with a sideswipe at her employer in her McTaggart lecture at the Edinburgh TV Festival, saying BBC impartiality too often amounted to "both-sidesism" – offering a false equivalence in the name of balance. Others have suggested personal political views should either be declared or should disqualify individuals from impartial reporting. But such verdicts are based on common misunderstanding about what those

terms mean and take little notice of what the public want from news providers.

Research by The Reuters Institute at Oxford University suggests polarisation among news audiences is relatively low (particularly outside the USA) and that, although news consumers recognise they are often drawn to partial news and opinion, all age groups spoke of the importance of impartial journalism. Focus group participants said they wanted a reliable baseline of factual reporting from which they could go off to explore opinions elsewhere in places where they expect to find them – social media, blogs, newspaper columns.

Many confusions cloud this debate. First, the widespread view that impartiality means false equivalence or "both-sidesism" or failing to call out the truth of a situation. Although there are some egregious examples of news programmes falling into that trap, it is not the benchmark for impartiality. They are examples of weak or poor journalism. Impartiality does not prevent the "calling out" of an issue – but it does require showing the rigorous evidence that sits behind that judgment; gathering evidence being harder work and a lot more expensive than a talking head in a studio.

Neither does impartiality mean hiding personal opinions or a pretence you don't hold any. It is the exact opposite of that. Impartiality is a professional discipline designed precisely to take account of personal bias and raise journalism above it. (Which is also, of course, harder work than letting your personal views run free.) Impartiality is not about the individual, it is about the process and method – something which news providers have been too reticent to explain.

In any case, disclosure of personal views – the frequent call for personal transparency – is not an answer and certainly cannot disqualify anyone from reporting. If personal views and experience are crucial to legitimacy, should only women report the abortion debate? Should that be only women who've had an abortion or only those

who haven't? Their different views are crucial to the debate, but the independent discipline of reporting and the martialling of evidence, including a range of views, should come first.

I recently spoke to a young Asian journalist who asked how they could be expected to cover racism impartially – or genocide? They assumed impartiality meant a "for and against" false equivalence. It doesn't. First-hand reporting and evidence enables strong, committed, impartial journalism. Show, don't just tell.

Simon Schama once suggested that "the certainty of an ultimately observable, empirically verifiable truth" was dead. He was writing about history of course. I am less pessimistic.

There are many kinds of truth – literal, metaphorical, artistic, relative or personal – but we should start with facts. My football team lost 1-0 is a fact. Why they lost can be the subject of debate. But the score is not an opinion. So let's start with facts. Report first, talk later.

We need a greater emphasis on a journalism of verification, not just assertion – let alone assumption. As the US scholar Tom Rosenstiel put it: "If journalists replace a flawed understanding of objectivity by taking refuge in subjectivity and think their opinions have more moral integrity than genuine inquiry, journalism will be lost." ✖

Richard Sambrook is former director of BBC News and Emeritus professor at Cardiff University

51(04):68/69|DOI:10.1177/03064220221144914

UK law risks criminalising the innocent

Arguably the most draconian piece of legislation out of the UK in decades, the Public Order Bill has no justification and could tear the fabric of British democratic life, says **DANNY SHAW**

ABOVE: A Just Stop Oil protester is arrested in London during a demonstration on 29 October this year. New legislation would not only criminalise environmental protesters on the UK's streets, it would criminalise potential protesters

CREDIT: Andrea Domeniconi/Alamy

AT MY LOCAL doctors' surgery in London, a receptionist walked in, late for work. A journey which should have taken her an hour had lasted twice as long, she said, because climate change protesters had climbed the gantries on the M25, the capital's orbital motorway.

For the safety of the activists and those driving beneath them, traffic had been diverted onto other roads, causing miles of tailbacks. "It was a right pain," she said.

She is not the only one to have been inconvenienced by Just Stop Oil, a group which is campaigning to stop new fossil fuel licensing and production. Job interviews have been missed, children have been late for school and hospital visits have been postponed.

And worse, Tony Bambury, from Buckinghamshire, was stuck in a jam when he should have been at his father's funeral. "I will never, ever forgive these people for what they've done to me," he told the BBC.

The controversy around the protests came to a head in the second week of November when a police motorcyclist was struck by a lorry as he attempted to marshal the congested traffic. Politicians urged police to take a firmer line. "That is your duty," home secretary Suella Braverman told officers at a policing conference, describing the environmentalists as "extremists" and the disruption as a "threat to our way of life".

Why was Braverman using such emotive language? Part of the reason, I suggest, is that she is attempting to sow division between her supporters and the "woke" critics of her Public Order Bill – government legislation that would significantly and dangerously extend the reach of law enforcement over protest groups.

The explanation for the bill on the Home Office website makes it sound benign – it is anything but. According to the department, the new laws will tackle "guerrilla" protest tactics which halt public transport networks, disrupt fuel supplies and prevent people (such as my doctor's receptionist) getting to work. If the measures are passed by parliament, it will be a crime for people to cause "serious disruption" by attaching themselves to objects, buildings or other people. Tunnelling will be criminalised and interference with major rail projects and key national infrastructure outlawed, too.

The measures are unnecessary. Police already have a panoply of powers to control events that cause serious disruption – and they have been used extensively during the Just Stop Oil action over the last year. Since October, London's Metropolitan Police alone

> **She is attempting to sow division between her supporters and the "woke" critics of her Public Order Bill**

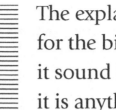

The explanation for the bill makes it sound benign – it is anything but

"criminalising" the innocent.

They are alarmed about plans to extend the police's ability to stop and search people for items used in protests such as glue, paint and locks. Stop-and-search is a highly contentious police tactic which is disproportionately deployed against those from Black and mixed ethnic communities. The committee believes that there is a risk the new expanded powers will be misused, including in a "discriminatory" manner that will have a "chilling effect" on the right to protest.

Its strongest criticism, however, is correctly directed at the proposed introduction of Serious Disruption Prevention Orders, which would allow the courts to ban people from going to specific places and meeting named individuals in order to prevent protest-related offences. Those subject to an SDPO might be required to wear an electronic tag and could be jailed if they breach the terms of an order.

The new court orders bear a troubling resemblance to terrorism prevention and investigation measures – known as T-Pims – which are designed to restrict and monitor the activities of terror suspects. Where national security is concerned, that is an appropriate and proportional response. Where protests are simply annoying, disruptive and cause people to be late for work, it is not.

If anything is a "threat to our way of life" it is the Public Order Bill itself. ✖

Danny Shaw is a commentator on policing, crime and justice and a former BBC Home Affairs correspondent

have made well over 700 arrests and brought charges against 150 people.

There are other legal options as well. Organisations which are affected by protests can apply for civil injunctions to prevent disruptive activity, with those in breach facing imprisonment for contempt of court. National Highways (which is responsible for major roads in England), councils in Essex, Transport for London and Shell are among those to have taken advantage.

And if that wasn't enough, consider the Police, Crime, Sentencing and Courts Act which became law in England and Wales only this year. The legislation gives police greater powers to place conditions on protests if the noise they generate could result in serious disruption, creates a statutory office of "public nuisance", and increases penalties for obstructing roads. In fact, the ink had barely dried on the act when the government introduced the Public Order Bill.

The Joint Committee on Human Rights, which comprises parliamentarians from the Conservative, Labour, SNP and Liberal Democrat parties, has articulated the concerns many of us have about the bill. It is not merely unnecessary, they say, but poses an "unacceptable threat to the fundamental right to engage in peaceful protest" and risks

51(04):70/71|DOI:10.1177/03064220221144915

Jennings

Our cartoonist turns his hand to how the media handles monarchy

51(04):72/73|DOI:10.1177/03064220221144916

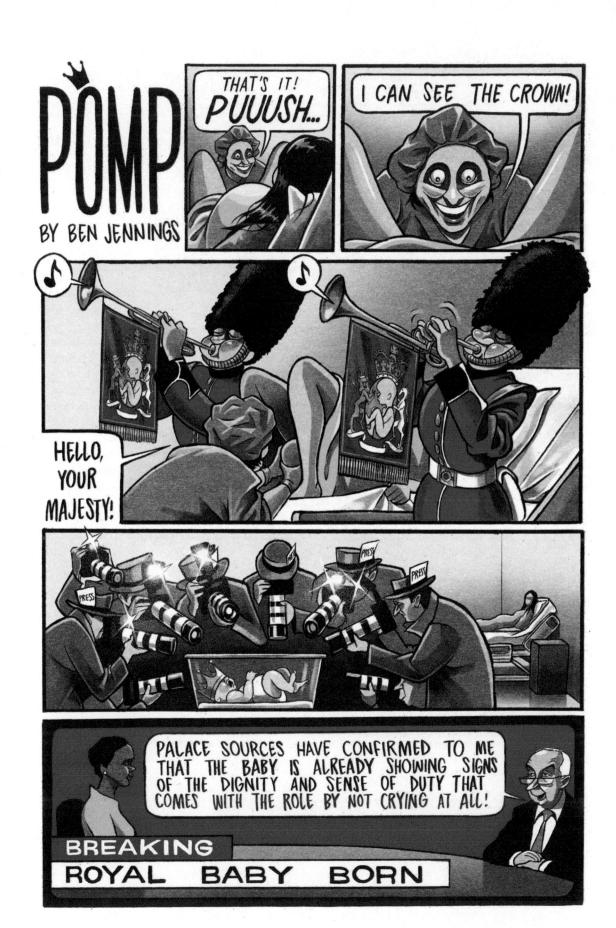

BEN JENNINGS:
an award-winning
cartoonist for The
Guardian and The
Economist whose
work has been
exhibited around
the world

GLOBAL VIEW

Challenge the gatekeepers

We can't keep kicking important free expression debates into the long grass, argues **RUTH ANDERSON**

SINCE THE PANDEMIC started I have become addicted to the spoken word. From the radio to audiobooks to podcasts, I typically find peace listening to others reading or debating. In recent weeks my latest addiction is a history podcast which has explored every issue from Justianian & Theodora to the Battle of Trafalgar to the impact of James Bond. In each episode the historians inevitably end up touching on the issue of freedom of expression, the role of propaganda, the impact of the printing press or the role of language in conflict. Because the reality is debates around freedom of expression have been a mainstay of our geo-political world for generations.

What is clear is that freedom of expression as a concept has rarely been easy. Regardless of the historical context and associated issues, each culture or community has their own view, each country their own application and each government their own definition. As communications and technology have evolved so has the debate about what is freedom of expression, what needs to be protected, where the lines are and how it is used both at home and abroad - when speech can become a diplomatic weapon.

Since our founding 50 years ago Index on Censorship has been at the heart of these debates as we explore the lines between freedom of expression and hate speech; media freedom and propaganda; academic freedom and respect or tolerance of views and opinions; publishing versus social media. In a world that is increasingly divided, where words are used as armaments and tyrants increasingly attempt to shape the external as well as internal dominant narrative the debate around what is and what is not freedom of expression has been all the more relevant. Which in turn makes Index's work all the more important.

 Whose job is it to make sure that freedom of expression is protected on every platform, online and offline?

LEFT: Maria Ressa at the Deutsche Welle Global Media Forum in June

Such accounts are reportedly being blocked, while parody and satire accounts more broadly now have to come with that label or face sanction

In November, former Index on Censorship Award judge (and recipient of the Nobel Peace Prize) Maria Ressa stated in the British media that: "free speech can be used to stifle free speech". She is of course right. Some people's voices overpower others. Some people have platforms that ensure they are heard when others are silenced. Some people use their own freedoms to dismantle the infrastructure that supports the freedoms of others. Governments have the power to limit media freedom and curtail access to the internet and social media platforms daily use algorithms to promote and restrict specific voices. And on too many occasions these collective restrictions are justified as efforts to protect freedom of expression.

Daily people attempt to justify why their human rights supersede others. Why they have the right to offend minority communities but those same communities do not have the right to protest about being offended. Why they shouldn't be cancelled but someone else should be. Some of the most entertaining debates on social media are when activists or commentators attempt to justify why their opinions have more value than someone else's, apparently forgetting that freedom of expression is a universal human right and does not include the right not be offended.

In recent weeks these arguments, especially on social media, have been compounded by the words and deeds of the new owner of Twitter, Elon Musk. His approach to free speech is apparently absolute, something Index would usually applaud but in this instance his commitment to it doesn't quite ring true. Because for Musk free speech can face removal if the account is making fun of him. Such accounts are reportedly being blocked, while parody and satire accounts more broadly now have to come with that

label or face sanction. And in an effort to make Twitter profitable accounts will now have the 'opportunity' to purchase a verified account, but even this has become farcical with people buying other's names and using them to promote misinformation, including about free medication in the USA. Musk's dream of a free speech utopia has quickly started to flounder upon being exposed to real life.

So what is the answer in the 21st century to how we promote, celebrate and protect freedom of speech? It's a question that has never felt more urgent to answer.

In an age when the world moves so quickly and is becoming increasingly divided, we need a level of pragmatism and a meeting of minds. We need a national and international conversation about what the lines of free speech are - or should be - and how, or if, they should vary depending on context and environment. Universities should be temples of debate, for sure, with unfettered free speech when debating and trying to understand the big issues of the day. Academic freedom relies on that precise principle. Social media, on the other hand, is more challenging. We might need to accept some social norms - especially on hate speech, misinformation and propaganda.

So we need to collectively decide, what do we want to protect? Whose voices should be heard? How do we want to amplify speech? Where is speech to be completely protected and where do we need to make compromises? And most importantly whose job is it to make sure that freedom of expression is protected on

every platform, online and offline? It's only then that we will be able to have a better appreciation of why freedom of expression needs to be protected in the 21st century, and how we can make sure that this most vital of human rights is cherished by those that need it most going forward.

One final word: Our last edition of the magazine had a special feature on the Football World Cup 2022 and how football is being used to sportswash the human rights records of tyrannical and despotic regimes. As I write today the Qatar World Cup is underway and every fear that human rights activists and organisations had about FIFA's decision to host the event in Qatar have come to fruition. Peaceful protests have been banned, the national teams threatened with sport sanctions if they demonstrate solidarity with minority groups. Clothing guidance has been issued and journalists have been threatened.

On this occasion, however, the leadership of Qatar (and of FIFA) have attempted to use a football contest not to improve their global reputation (as we thought they would) but rather as an effort to normalise authoritarianism. This cannot stand. The decisions taken by FIFA and Qatar to undermine our collective human rights to freedom of expression and the right to protest cannot and must not be tolerated. FIFA have discredited world football and as we move forward they must be held to account for their actions both during the tournament and in the aftermath. ✖

Ruth Anderson is CEO of Index

51(04):74/75|DOI:10.1177/03064220221144917

YOU HAVE NOT YET BEEN DEFEATED

You Have Not Yet Been Defeated by Alaa Abd El-Fattah is a book about the importance of ideas, whatever their cost.

'What can any one person do with a legacy of pain, struggle and courage? There are no easy solutions here, but *You Have Not Yet Been Defeated* is a heartbreaking, hopeful answer.' — Rachel Aspden, *Guardian*

Available from all good bookshops and fitzcarraldoeditions.com

Fitzcarraldo Editions

CULTURE

"We knew we were followed and some were reported but nothing happened. Because it was fiction, satirical stuff"

ANDREY KURKOV | THE UNBEATEN | P.92

Russia's exiled author writes back

ZINOVY ZINIK talks to **MARTIN BRIGHT** about broadcasting for the BBC and how publishing remains one of the last free spaces in Putin's Russia

ABOVE: The writer
Zinovy Zinik

ZINOVY ZINIK IS not easy to define. He is a Russian novelist and short story writer who has written all his best-known works while living in exile. He writes mainly in his native language, but sometimes prefers to express himself in English – as in His Master's Voice, the story published exclusively in this edition of Index. He was able to escape the Soviet Union to Israel in 1975 because of his Jewish family origins (his real family name is Gluzberg), but he was not brought up in the Jewish faith. As an opponent of the regime, he had his Soviet citizenship stripped from him, but dislikes the term "dissident".

His portraits of the lives of exiled intellectuals brought him to prominence in Britain in the 1990s, when his novel, The Mushroom Picker, was made into a series for BBC television. But in the years after the collapse of the Soviet Union, he became increasingly popular in Russia itself. His latest publication, from which His Master's Voice is taken, is a vast 700-page collection of stories from the past 40 years published in Moscow under the title No Cause for Alarm — somewhat ironic in the present circumstances.

Zinik tells me there is a motif running through all the stories in the collection of the individual trapped within an enclosed space. "This enclosed space might be physical. It could be a lift or could be a carriage with its doors shut. Or it could even be the loo. But it could be locked into certain personal circumstances."

As he saw this motif returning time and again in his work, Zinik asked himself why this real or symbolic claustrophobia was haunting him and realised it went back to his sense of people being trapped in the collectivist, Marxist ideology of the Soviet Union.

"They have been bombarded by the idea that our personality is the product of external circumstances. But I think, to use an old biblical quotation from Exodus, 'Thou shalt not follow a multitude to do evil'. And I always worry about any collective notion, or the multitude obsessed with a certain idea," he said.

For Zinik, a person can only find their true identity when they are tested by confronting some form of imprisonment. "You have to find some resources, some roots inside you that are your real self and not some perception of you by a collective."

His Master's Voice is inspired by his many decades in exile as a radio journalist for the BBC, especially his time at the Russian section of the World Service. "My life was divided into my physical presence here and only my voice would reach my old friends and family. So, my voice became a kind of soul. And this division is a very vulnerable one because you can lose your voice in many ways."

Zinik said the increasing severity of censorship in Russia has not yet extended to literary fiction but felt that "any deviation into the open political field would be immediately noticed".

"Generally speaking, they still keep on publishing books, great books. What is really amazing is that a lot of editors are now on the run, but because of the electronic age, they are still editing books, which are getting printed still in Russia."

However, the real problem was distribution. Zinik's publisher, New Literary Observer, struggled even to get copies of No Cause for Alarm sent to the author.

So how did 24 February affect him personally? "In a way, it was identical to what I felt in 1968 after the Soviet army's invasion of Czechoslovakia. It had an absolutely devastating effect on everyone with a bit of a brain."

The work of Zinovy Zinik provides a crucial link between the generation who experienced the reality of the Soviet Union and the tragedy provoked by those nostalgic for that time. His recurring motif of the trapped individual struggling to escape the collective mindset remains a powerful metaphor for Russia's predicament. ✖

Martin Bright is editor-at-large at Index on Censorship

> They have been bombarded by the idea that our personality is the product of external circumstances

His Master's Voice

Zinovy Zinik

I HAD NEVER been subjected to any kind of imprisonment in the totalitarian Soviet Russia where I was born and grew up; I had to emigrate to the West and become a vocal symbol of the Free World to be placed behind the bars fifty years later. The interrogation room in my current place of incarceration doesn't look essentially different from the Corporation's radio studio from which I, for the last fifty years, have been broadcasting to Russia. Like a radio studio, the cell is well insulated from any audible interference from the outside world. There is even a microphone, fixed to my lapel, for my replies to be recorded and analysed by my case officer as well as by the psychiatrist who sits behind a two-way mirror. Even this semi-transparent wall is not unlike the glass partition separating the sound engineer in the cubical from the broadcaster seated before his microphone. The broadcaster's voice is sent over the airwaves, reaching those regions of the world from which your physical appearance has been barred by the Iron Curtain for the major part of your life. During the Cold War years, my body was in the West while my voice was penetrating the Soviet jamming devices to reach listeners in the totalitarian East. We existed for Russia on the air only, voices in a bodiless state. In that sense, broadcasting, exile and imprisonment has always, for me, been one and the same thing. The Iron Curtain disappeared, but these prison bars will safely divide me from the rest of the world for some time yet.

Nowadays, my voice can reach the world only via my lawyer. But first, it is filtered through the ears of my investigator and the psychiatrist. The psychiatrist eavesdrops on my conversation with the case officer. The reason for the psychiatrist's presence is that my lawyer insists I should plead diminished responsibility in order to reduce my murder conviction to manslaughter. But I don't want to pretend to be some kind of a mentally-challenged nutcase with the diminished brainpowers. I committed murder in full mental capacity. I bear full responsibility for my actions and, given a chance, I would do it again.

The psychiatrist is convinced I hear voices in my head. But he doesn't comprehend the nature of radio work. It is the listener who hears voices in his head—the voices that we broadcast via transmitters. And the voice is no doubt symbolic of the soul, its shadow. The Corporation's contract stipulates that you must hand over your vocal identity to its organisation—a kind of unconditional surrender, which emulates the Gothic fairy tale about the man who sold his shadow to the powers of darkness. I am trying to explain to the case officer the story of my voice, lost and regained. It was stolen from me, and came back in a different disguise.

The beginning of the story coincides with the decision of the administration to get rid of me. Nora Bluntik, our Department Head, invited me to her spacious office for, "an informal preliminary chit-chat," as she put it in her mail, about a possible termination of my life-long collaboration with the Corporation. When I entered the room, she looked at me like a grandma would at her naughty grandchild, masking her malicious intentions with a toothy smile, jaded and hypocritical. Her manly suit and high heels were as charming as a tortoise's shell. She always exuded an icy corporate charm mixed with a whiff of camphor.

During the Cold War years, Nora Bluntik used to present the station's music programme where she gave audio dance lessons on the samba, cha-cha-cha and other moves learnt during her youth spent in a North London suburb. The Corporation's bosses were convinced that in Soviet Russia the only dance technique taught to the population was energetic marching across Red Square to the accompaniment of a military brass band. Now, with the same well-trained enthusiasm, as if she was executing the pirouette of a samba dancer, Nora Bluntik tried to convince me—in the presence of the administration's lawyer—to accept the golden handshake, the size of which had never previously been offered →

→ to anyone. They were bribing me, "one of the most outstanding broadcasters in the Russian language," as she put it, and praising me hypocritically in a bid to convince me to leave the Corporation quietly and without fuss. Others, the so-called "most outstanding ones" had long gone; their souls crossed through the ether to the other side, to travel indefinitely in the frictionless void of darkness where the stars are as silent as fish in an aquarium.

These days in the shadowy corridors of the Corporation, youngsters with insolent smiles on their spotted faces loiter with intent. They are the newly employed broadcasters from post-Soviet Russia imported by Nora Blutnik, the great enthusiast of all revolutions in the world—should they happen, that is, a safe distance from her cosseted suburban home. I have no doubts whatsoever that all these new Russian employees were once professional journalists in Soviet Russia. Behind Bluntik's chair hangs a portrait of Sir Obadiah Gershwin, the patriarch of broadcasting to Russia. I had noticed that for some time now, the smile with which Sir Obadiah Gershwin had been observing the goings-on beneath him was no longer an expression of benevolent irony but squeamish revulsion.

At my meeting with Nora Bluntik, I was paralysed with an identical squeamish grimace. She was obviously instructed by her superior to inform me about the Corporation's great leap into the electronic digital age. I listened to her gobbledygook about virtual reality and interactive websites, about audience-generated content and internet broadcasts, direct messaging from mobile phones and aggressive audio interactions with the use of simultaneous live recording, and it was clear to me she didn't understand a modicum of

Youngsters with insolent smiles on their spotted faces loiter with intent

this technological drivel. The inevitable conclusion one should draw from listening to this poppycock was clear to both of us. I had been observing Nora's shifty eyes, her toothy smile distorted by her verbal cha-cha-chas, her demagogic tricks and other sambas of bullshitting, employed in order to fuck up and paralyse my intellect. Out of this fog of audible rubbish two points eventually emerged. Since I was rapidly approaching the age of retirement, and bearing in mind my manifest aversion to the digital innovations in broadcasting, I was considered by the Corporation a relic of a bygone epoch. If the content of a broadcast is generated by the audience, the necessity of the broadcaster is annulled. My forty years of broadcasting had gone to the dogs. I was like an item from the Corporation's cabinet of curiosities of the Cold War.

Indeed, I was the only one at the Corporation who still used an antiquated editing machine for my recordings. A traditional tape recorder stood proudly next to my desk: I've never used computerised editing technique. My desk with its letter trays, a stack of writing paper, stapler and a box of rubber bands looked like a museum installation. Apart from me, and the administration, everyone else at the Corporation was hot-desking, a system whereby no one has a fixed place of work, but instead occupies any free desk available at any given moment. You start by depriving a person of his individual place; you end with him losing his individuality as a displaced person. But in a world where no one is irreplaceable—as Joseph Stalin was fond of saying—there is no such a thing as individuality. You have a broken heart? We'll replace it.

Bastards.

A mutual agreement about my early retirement was reached and signed by me and Nora Bluntik in private and in silence. A massive golden handshake sealed my lips. My mouth was jammed with money. In protest, I've sealed my ears. Back home, I've switched off my radio, not to switch it on ever again. Why should I listen to the optimistic drivel of semi-educated radio mercenaries polluting

CREDIT: Iruchka Karzanova

Had I sold my soul and my voice to the new oligarchic elite and the Moscow ruling mafia?

→ the airwaves with their badly-digested ideas and demonstrative populism, cultural mumbo-jumbo, verbal sambas and ideological cha-cha-cha. I was glad my voice was no longer mixed in with these sticky audible substances.

So I thought. Fairly soon after my retirement, however, I was baffled when my former loyal admirers started pestering me with telephone and postal messages, expressing their alarm at my recent broadcasts. They informed me that my voice was the same and as charming as ever, the very one they so much admired, but the content of my broadcasts was totally unbecoming for my honourable reputation. Nobody would ever have imagined, they said, that I, an ironical liberal freethinker, with my encyclopaedic knowledge of world affairs, would bend the ears of my listeners with populist drivel about motherland, native soil, blood bond and God. How and when, my bewildered admirers enquired, did I make a complete u-turn in my political orientation? Had I sold my soul and my voice to the new oligarchic elite and the Moscow ruling mafia?

I was shocked. It was absurd. The Corporation was no longer my employer. I was not part of its output. I couldn't broadcast any reactionary trash over its radio waves, since my voice had been cut out and my recording tapes removed into their dustbins of history. My voice could no longer be heard on the radio because I lost it – the voice.

I lost my voice a couple of months before my forced retirement. I mean, I'd lost it quite literally. That's the reason why I was silent when I had signed the retirement agreement. Even if I wanted to contradict the nonsense that Nora Bluntik had been stuffing into my ears, nobody would have heard me. I looked like a fish, floating in the dark water of an aquarium, forever opening its mouth but emitting no sound. Yes, the trouble with my throat had been aggravating speedily for some time before my confrontation with Nora Bluntik. The loss of voice was a good enough excuse for her to get rid of the veteran broadcaster.

I remember the first symptoms of it. I didn't sneeze or cough. I had no flu or lung disease. One Monday I felt some tightness in my throat and my voice became hoarse and croaky. By Thursday, the day of my weekly broadcasts, the quality of my voice had deteriorated so drastically that the studio manager's assistant ran to the canteen for a cup of hot milk and honey to repair my broken vocal chords. Hot milk didn't help. Neither did such home recipes as hot toddies, breathing gymnastics over the evaporation of the boiling potatoes, or the use of earplugs during the night's sleep. For a while my listeners might have thought I had been replaced by Tom Waits speaking Russian. Gradually, my mouth started to issue into the microphone sounds reminiscent of a scratched vinyl record, or more like an out of tune radio receiver emitting crackling and hissing instead of words. In Moscow, I was informed, my Russian listeners, who live permanently in a paranoid atmosphere of political conspiracies, had decided that the Russian government might have considered the reintroduction of jamming. I had no choice but take some days off and seek medical help.

I was referred by my GP to the local hospital's Ear, Nose & Throat department, where a specialist with a huge periscope looked into the depths of my throat by introducing, via my nostril, a thin tube with a light bulb at the end. By such invasive means, he was able to establish that there was no alien creature dwelling down there. The doctor then showed me the colour print of the insides of my throat. I must confess, what I saw resembled vaginal folds in a state of erotic arousal. No wonder the psychiatrist, attached to my criminal case, recently tried to investigate my familiarity with oral sex in my adolescence years, as well as other aspects of my uncertain sexual orientation. The word 'psychosomatic' was mentioned.

The doctor gave me some lozenges to suck and

a set of seven straws for breathing exercises. She advised me to blow through one straw every day as if it was a trumpet, simultaneously contracting my belly muscles. I grabbed these straws as a drowning man might, but my voice didn't come back. Was it snatched by some bacilli? These mysterious ailments, if they don't go away on their own volition, stay forever, regardless of how you treat them—just like drunken Russian guests. Every morning, I looked in the mirror to see the familiar features of my ageing face but when I opened my mouth, I couldn't recognize my voice: instead, a monstrous stranger hissed maliciously back at me. I attempted to explain away my handicap to my acquaintances by telling a Baron Munchausen's story about my trip to Russia as a broadcaster, where my voice got frozen and hung, as it were, in the air so I couldn't extract it and put it back into my mouth, and so returned to London voiceless. I was a joke, of course, because I had not been to Russia since the day of my emigration to the West nearly half a century ago.

Not many people, though, were willing to listen to my predicament, since I could now express myself only by erratic and barely distinguishable syllables. The truth is that like the man without a shadow, the one without voice is shunned and ignored by fellow humans. The man without a shadow seeks places where fog or dimness blurs the border between light and darkness so his lack of shadow is not immediately noticeable. Similarly, I began to frequent noisy pubs where nobody could hear anyone because of the deafening music, and everyone communicated through gestures only. That suited me well. I began drinking heavily, but the clarity of my mind had not been impaired.

* * *

THE INVESTIGATOR RETURNS again and again to the same point of inquiry: why was it that during the encounter with my victim did I happen to have a razor in my pocket? My interrogator pressed this point in order to prove that the murder had been premeditated. I kept on explaining again and again to my investigator,

who is a computerised person of the digital age, that as a broadcaster I used to work not with digital files but with tapes and material objects. I belonged to that generation of broadcasters who edited tapes mechanically, cutting out unwanted sections with an editing razor and splicing ends together with transparent scotch. Once upon a time, these editing razors were kept in open boxes in every office and they were available to everyone. Each razor was encased in a kind of cardboard wrapping and easily snapped open. Editors like me had quite a few of them kept casually in our pockets, ready to use when needed. I used such a razor in an attempt to recreate my voice artificially.

Having gone temporarily silent but not yet forced into retirement by the Corporation, I decided to listen to my old archive recordings when my voice had been good and fair. I was enjoying the nostalgic sound of my old self, my velvety baritone, and it felt like being simultaneously my own Echo, and Narcissus too, hearing in these tapes an audible reflection of my personality. I should consider, I thought, cutting up my old recordings into separate words and readymade miniature blocks, from which a new broadcast can be pasted together each time I needed it. Like Dr Frankenstein who created his Monster by stitching together bits and pieces of dead flesh, I would create an ideal version of my speech by sticking together bits of live recording. After all, the spoken life of an individual consists of a set of clichés, so that from these prefabricated bits one could construct any sentence fancied, with proper pauses in between. In the audio archives of the Corporation there is even a section labelled 'Pauses'. These 'pauses' are used to recreate certain atmospheres of a place, or to ➔

My interrogator pressed this point in order to prove that the murder had been premeditated

→ link different bits of a tape as if they were recorded in the same place.

All these fanciful plans for restoring my vocal self were totally futile: my broadcasting days had been numbered. My voiceless self became a metaphorical archival pause of that kind.

It was one of those evenings when, still silent and already unemployed, I sat alone in my apartment and watched the soundless sunset over the noisy metropolis from my window. The landline telephone rang; I picked up the receiver and heard the sound of my own voice. It was so bizarre that at first I thought I was hearing my pre-recorded answering phone message. The voice on the line suggested that we should, if I didn't mind, meet up at the Corporation's bar. Would I be free this evening? Stunned and intrigued, I hissed something affirmative. The voice replied how glad he was to hear it. He would be eagerly anticipating me and waiting at table no. 101, the one near the fish tank.

The moment I appeared at the entrance to the bar, a young man jumped up from his seat and ran towards the door to greet me with excessive enthusiasm. Smiling almost obsequiously, he led me to my seat next to the fish tank. He ordered a large and expensive whisky: the Russians are proud to know the best labels of malt. I ordered my usual, a Bloody Mary, well aware the effect the spicy mixture would have on my irritated throat. Everything about his appearance was alien to me. His semi-shaved, piggish face had smatterings of trendy stubble. He was dressed as they all do these days: like an adolescent boy who had overgrown his old school uniform. Tight jacket, skinny jeans and pink sneakers instead of proper shoes. As it usually happens with those dedicated followers of fashion from Russia, their immaculate image   →

CREDIT: Iruchka Karzanova

→ was ruined by some erroneous detail. In this case it was his unbelievably preposterous glasses. Armani spectacles with a garish frame, studded with fake diamonds and embellished at the corners with golden angelic wings made of plastic. He exuded a rehearsed ease in his manners, but it was immediately clear that once he had your attention, it wouldn't be easy to break free. The moment you saw him, generic as his face was, it was impossible to wipe his intrusive and unpleasant features from your memory, whatever feeling one had hearing his voice. And his voice, as I said, was absolutely identical to mine. It was a horrifying revelation that my voice could be identified as that of the person sitting in front of me now.

Having scrutinised his face at leisure, I realised that I had seen the man before. I didn't remember the exact circumstances, but it must have been somewhere in the corridors of the Corporation. Since the collapse of Communism, so-called "visitors from Moscow" had been meandering around our offices unhindered, observing our work, watching me at my desk and in front of the microphone through the glass partition of the studio manager's cubicle, rather like I was an exotic fish. I refused to be photographed. In my era of broadcasting, there were no websites packed with publicity photos of broadcasters. I used to be the invisible man with a magic voice reaching Russia from behind the Iron Curtain.

As if eavesdropping on these very thoughts, my host told me, with sycophantic reverence, that many years ago at the early stages of his professional life, my anonymity had inspired him and his mates to try imagine what I looked like. Avid listeners of my broadcasts, they debated whether I resembled a Victorian scientist dressed

So-called "visitors from Moscow" had been meandering around our offices unhindered

in tweeds, or perhaps a Wildean bohemian with a green carnation in his lapel. Others of his compatriots pictured me as Sherlock Holmes with his familiar pipe or a retired general with a waxed handlebar moustache. My interlocutor, who introduced himself as Victor Chertkoff, was now observing intensely every aspect of my outward appearance as if I was a museum exhibit.

In reality, I did not in the least resemble any of the English gentlemen they pictured. As the years progressed, my paunch had grown bigger and my baldness more and more prominent, creating a steep and shining forehead similar to that of Sir Obadiah Gershwin, the Corporation's founding father. In the later part of my life I had become fond of light grey suits and brogues that Sir Obadiah used to wear. Gradually, I would, like him, stick to the habit of donning a bow tie. I knew that my colleagues sniggered at my old-fashioned appearance, calling me Sir Obadiah's doppelganger behind my back. They spread malicious gossip about me as a usurper of his manner of speech. He would talk into the microphone as if he was delivering a stage soliloquy, carefully articulating every word in rhythmic cadences. Sir Obadiah understood the role that the diaphragm plays in the work of the broadcaster. I followed all these mannerisms impeccably. I have polished and improved his method.

And now, this puppet—this cheeky Russian upstart—was lecturing me on my vocal characteristics. He was, of course, delighted to see me in person, face-to-face, he said. The invisibility of the broadcaster emancipates the listener's imagination, he said. Like in a science fiction novel, the disembodied voice acquires the shape and features which are dearest to the listener. It was exactly because nobody knew what I looked like that my appearance in people's imagination could assume any shape, form and style, he said. And therefore, paradoxically, my real appearance was irrelevant. Anonymous in appearance, as all members of the Corporation, we were also strongly discouraged from making any personal statements live on air. My personality was incorporated. Does it really matter who the broadcaster is in real life? Does it really matter what he says? The only real aspect of the broadcaster is his voice. And since our voices are identical, people might even think—following Mr. Chertkoff's logic—that I looked like him. (I visibly shuddered at this suggestion). And this is very important, he repeated, for our project. Which project? Our project? I was bewildered, but didn't say a word, just opened my mouth in a silent question mark, waiting for him to elaborate.

My voice was, of course, legendary in Russia. He grew up listening to my voice emanating from radio receivers in every decent household in Moscow. Days and nights, nonstop, he kept on trying to hone his voice to be indistinguishable from mine, tracing every turn and twist of my vocal delivery. By that time he was a mature graduate of the school for professional radio journalists, with a considerable experience in the Soviet media, busy disseminating mass disinformation.

And then, a few months ago, something happened. He remembered the date: Labour Day, the first of May of two thousand and eleven. He came to the studio of the World Service of Radio Russia, opened the microphone and the producer immediately ordered the studio manager to stop the broadcasting. They thought that somehow the Corporation's radio waves had infiltrated and overtaken the Russian broadcasting system and that it was I, not him, with my voice from London, speaking directly to the Russian listeners!

Shocked myself, but silent, I registered in my mind the date of his transformation (or epiphany). It was the very date when Nora Bluntik managed to remove me from the broadcasting schedule, using the chronic loss of my voice as a pretext. It gradually had been dawning on me as to where my voice might have gone: into Mr. Chertkoff's voice box. One shouldn't be surprised too much at the absolute similarity of our voices, my vocal doppelganger said, because our voices are no longer unique and irreplaceable. It was useless for me to argue with him, telling him that for me the voice was a physical extension of my personality, like my hand, or my eye or my ear; it is inseparable from me.

No, one should not be too sentimental about

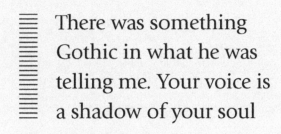

There was something Gothic in what he was telling me. Your voice is a shadow of your soul

it, he retorted. Your voice ceases to be part of you the moment it leaves your lips. Via microphone, it travels by the cable to the transmitter that spreads it all over the world to be recorded, copied and disseminated in audio files and many other formats. It no longer belongs to you individually, it could be multiplied and broadcast by the push of a button. Different radio personalities can use that voice as their own. There was something Gothic in what he was telling me. Your voice is a shadow of your soul, and its audio copy—like an echo—is a shadow of your voice. The Corporation trades in the shadows of its broadcasters. One such shadow was sitting in front of me, pontificating about something sinister he kept on calling our project.

We both, as he put it, belonged to the school of the speech delivery as developed by the inimitable Sir Obadiah Gershwin. He meant Sir Obadiah's stage-like manner of talking into the microphone, his Oxbridge accent. Politically neutral by nature, this manner of speech was a *lingua franca* that liberated the broadcaster from his complicated past, his complex origin and political affiliations. The manifested neutrality of that mode of speech was, according Mr. Chertkoff, the essence of universalism, humanism and tolerance— cornerstones of the free world. That's why even ordinary Russian housewives would stop in the middle of cooking their borscht in order to listen to your broadcasts, he said.

I kept on listening to his overblown praise of my radio work, trying to uncover a hidden motive behind his obsequious paeans to my broadcasting gifts. Too much attention is paid to the significance of words, Mr. Chertkoff said, to the meaning of what one says. Is the content of one's speech really important? One day →

I was boiling up with inner rage, but only capable of moving my mouth silently

→ we say one thing, but tomorrow we say the opposite, with the same intensity and no lesser conviction. We are familiar with these perennial inconsistencies without consciously realising them. It's like with medical opinions: one day they declare the thing lethal, the next day they say it's essential for longevity. And we obediently follow such idiotic and self-contradictory advice, so long as we believe the person who advises us. A private doctor in the nineteenth century was paid for his reassuring bedside manner, all the while proscribing his patient nothing stronger than an innocent placebo. Our faith in a doctor depends not on what he says, but how he says it: the tone of his voice and the voice itself. By having a voice and intonation identical to yours, he said, we would simply refill its message with new content without diminishing its effect. The people of Russia would swallow the whole— hook, line and sinker—with the same enthusiasm they'd been nourishing every sound bite of Sir Obadiah in the past!

Shush! Shush! Reacting to the nervous twitching of my mouth in my efforts to raise voiceless objections, he stretched his hand in front of my face like a policeman barring entrance. Whatever you want to say, I will say it for you. I am your voice! He said this brazenly, knowing that I was unable to utter a squeak. I was boiling up with inner rage, but only capable of moving my mouth silently, in a fish-like manner, with my lips distorted, caught between an icy smile and a grimace of revulsion. Then he said something that made me shudder. They've been thinking for some time now of getting rid of the likes of you, he said.

I leaned back in my chair, paralysed. He started to elaborate, pacing his sentences rhythmically and in a well-balanced way, but at the same time with authority and resolution. According to Chertkoff, my generation of broadcasters with our subtle irony, diffident scepticism, and our ardent defence of civil liberties, had created a climate in which ideologically provocative ideas were encouraged. These irresponsible broadcasts might bend the fragile moral staples that underpin the spiritual life of newly born, post-Soviet Russia. According to Mr. Cherkoff, my well-balanced voice sounded, to Russian listeners, like the Trumpets of Jericho knocking the country off her feet in a historical moment when she'd just risen up from her knees. Chertkoff declared that his mission was to save me, personally, and the process of liberalisation of Russia, in general.

It turns out that my informers were right when they had warned me that somebody in Moscow was using my voice to broadcast ideas totally alien to my worldview. Chertkoff was clearly not alien to those ideas. Yes, he said, but there is nothing wrong with an idea per se, even if it sounds like a fascist idea. It is not the idea, but its implementation that matters. And such an implementation depends on who is interpreting that idea. But you wouldn't compare Hitler with Shakespeare, he said, although the latter was also talking about the native soil and blood bonds, as did Heidegger or Emil Chioran. One would not dare to repeat in a polite society certain ideas that the Russian genius Dostoevsky had propagated during certain periods of his miserable life. One cannot demand from all of us to be like Emmanuel Levinas or Simone Weil! It would be better if he, an enlightened broadcaster, rather than some freak with his crypto-Nazi views from Mars, aired the ideas of national roots, blood bonds and religious orthodoxy. Because we cannot pretend any longer that these, "so-called fascist ideas are just temporary delusions instigated by some lunatics." Ordinary people, hoi-polloi, the populace, are the real rulers of the new social media, expressing themselves by 'liking' whatever they fancy on Facebook, fed up with the liberal establishment and its strictures of political correctness, with victims of colonialism and sexual minorities. They are fed up with our irony, moral ambivalence and theological paradoxes. Ordinary people don't want to be affiliated with a sceptical minority of dissident liberals. They want to belong to something bigger than themselves, to preach ideals that are rooted in something firm and permanent, in a collective power and basic moral principles propped by the massive popular support and cheered by ever enthusiastic Facebookers. This transformation of public opinion is already irreversible and those who resist this historical momentum will be crushed under its wheels—with no one left to care about your unique personality, your personal uniqueness.

The individual is doomed to perish because he is the mortal one, Chertkoff continued. It is the collective that survives. And he finally put forward a proposal for which he evidently had planned in advance for me to hear. He suggested that we should initiate the process of 'collectivisation' of my legacy as a legendary broadcaster. He wanted me to grant him the full rights for the entire output of my radio work collected in the Corporation's archives. He would start rebroadcasting them with my lost voice (that is, with his own voice, identical to mine), but with some imperceptible modifications, changing the content ever so slightly here and there, giving it a different spin without altering the manner of delivery. He knows how to frame my ideas in such a way that not a single proto-Fascist activist in Russia would ever think of harming me as a dangerous libertine and degenerate. But the enlightening influence of my voice on the masses would be as strong as ever, because, he said, it is the intonation, those well-balanced cadences of my voice, that convey the real message. The inimitable, "on one hand … on the other hand," will resound forever, filling in between whatever is politically correct and demanded in the hour of need by the collective consciousness. While talking to me, Mr. Chertkoff took a sip of his malt whisky from a crystal glass the same way I used to sip water from time to time during my broadcasts.

Don't listen to him, don't listen to him, my inner voice kept on telling me. But I couldn't help but listen to him as if hypnotised. I heard my

voice, there was no mistake about it, but it was being taken from of me and put into somebody else's mouth. I wanted to prize his jaws open and to stare into his throat, to see the vaginal folds there that gave birth to these invasive sounds and intrusive thoughts, to analyse the mechanism of his larynx, his vocal chords, to find out how the person, whose features were so repulsive to me, was capable of issuing a voice so identical to mine. My mind was enraged by what it was saying, but my soul, inseparable from my voice, was succumbing to its tidal comings.

At this moment, he turned his attention away from me removing from his inside pocket some papers and a pen. The documents bore the Corporation's letterhead and looked like a copy of a formal contract. Catching now his face side on, I suddenly remembered where I had first encountered him. It was in the days before my departure from the Corporation, in the gents on the fifth floor, next to the recording studio. Due to the aging male's problems with the prostate and bladder, I had been taking a little time to detach myself from my place in front of the pisser's bowl, when another man moved in to relieve himself next to me. I tried, as we all do, not to glance aside, but my eye couldn't avoid the sight of his mighty tool. He quickly finished pissing with a jolly bursting noise, but instead of leaving he started masturbating, calmly and energetically. In no time I was made a witness to a powerful erection. I was aware that he knew, surely, that I was watching him. I could swear that under the cover of his faddish facial growth, an insolent and triumphant smile of a young and strong barbarian made its fleeting appearance.

The same imperceptible smile was again roaming his thin lips as we sat together now →

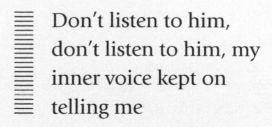

Don't listen to him, don't listen to him, my inner voice kept on telling me

→ in the bar. He took out his pen and laid out the contractual papers in front of me while prattling on non-stop, trying to convince me of the brilliance of his strategy. But I wasn't listening any longer. I had stopped listening for some time. Instead, I was staring at the fish tank next to our table. With his voice still droning on, I longed for silence and the fish were the only creatures in the entire building that were capable of being soundless. The ichthyologists would say that fish also talk: they communicate with one another on ultrasonic wavelengths. Or maybe on some other wavelength, I'm not too sure. The point is that as far as the human ear is concerned, fish are mute because we cannot hear them. This, to my mind, is their great gift to the world. Ah, silence is golden! I remained silent.

I remember how these fish looked in the golden old days, when the bar still resembled an English gentleman's club complete with worn leather armchairs, oak panelling, high ceilings and a whiff of cigar smoke clinging to the carpet. Back then, the aquarium stood proudly in the middle of the room with its tropical denizens, as exotic and delicate as rare butterflies, like emblems of the British Empire's rich colonial past. Only the rustle of newspapers and the clinking of ice in glasses disturbed their magical silence. But with the passing of time, the bar, too, succumbed to the onslaught of television monitors and their incessant din. Then the deafening pop-music was added to the noisy banter of drunken plebs. Remarkably, as the interior design of the bar grew more democratic and optimistic, the appearance and demeanour of the fish became ever dourer. Like the humans around them, they seemed to become more fretful, aggressive and agitated in response to the ambient cacophony.

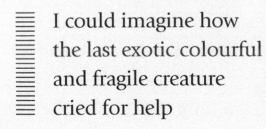

I could imagine how the last exotic colourful and fragile creature cried for help

But the real turning point came when half of the bar was separated off with a partition, behind which a gym was installed. The aquarium was also divided, with one of its glass sides looking out onto the noisy new generation of radio broadcasters at the bar and the other onto the broadcasters building up their muscles in the gym (perhaps in order to be able to hold heavy microphones more steadily, or to keep their mouths firmly shut). This event signalled the beginning of an irreversible metamorphosis in the aquarium. Suddenly the fish became markedly fewer in quantity, while appearing to grow individually in size. In other words, half of the fish tank was learning to socialise, while the other half was learning to work out. Which side would prevail?

Now I saw it all clearly. A handful of gigantic fish were circling the aquarium in moody silence. Grey scales glinting like gunmetal, they passed one another with sidelong glances of hatred, slowly opening their mouths as if to emit a string of foul expletives. Their eyes gleamed with the rapacious greed of pikes. And I understood that, under the influence of the surrounding environment, the fish in the aquarium had been devouring one another, evolving into a new cannibalistic breed. I could imagine how the last exotic colourful and fragile creature cried for help. Only humans might have helped it, but humans hear neither a fish's cries nor their laughter.

Having thus contemplated this silent metamorphosis, I've arrived to a striking conclusion. It dawned on me why all these newly-recruited professional employees of the Corporation—protégés of Nora Bluntik—had arrived under the disguise of the open international borders of the digital universe, of cultural cooperation, and all that poppycock. My free world, made up of different kinds of exotic and exuberantly colourful fish, was being invaded by the uniformly grey pikes of foreign propaganda.

Bastards.

Silently, I beckoned Mr. Chertkoff with my finger, inviting him to have a closer look at the denizens of the aquarium's muddy waters. I opened the top lid that is used for feeding the fish, prompting him with a gentle nudge to lean over the fish tank to observe the grey, scaly monsters moving around in a kingly fashion under the scum. He couldn't comprehend what I wanted of him, but for politeness' sake leaned with me over the aquarium edge, expressing a modicum of interest in its fishy content. Simultaneously, my right hand fumbled the contents of my side pocket; I traced and grasped firmly between my index finger and thumb a miniature razor blade that radiomen like me used for cutting and splicing audiotapes.

Without much ado—for he clearly didn't expect any violent gesture on my part—I grasped the back of his head with my left hand, bending his head slightly and, at the same time, deftly, with a single swift swipe of my right hand, slashed his throat with the razor blade.

He didn't have a chance to emit even the expected groan when I pushed his head face down into the fish tank, a solid construction on the cement base that didn't even shake. His hands embraced it as if he was about to dive in for a swim. Underwater, his face bore an expression of utter puzzlement. His half-open mouth emitted air bubbles that were greeted with the bubbles issued by the keen grey fishes as they rushed forwards hopeful of a new prey but immediately recoiled sensing an alien intrusion. I relished this encounter for a short while: my enemy, now dead, meeting the piscarius creatures of the aquarium that looked like his metaphoric doubles. Clouds of blood unravelling under the water made the fish retreat into the farthest corner of the aquarium. Like them, the drinkers around us stood up and silently moved away from me. They'd been staring at me in panic, as I stood in the middle of the bar with the miniature razor in my fingers, my sleeves sprinkled with the blood from my doppelganger's larynx, his vocal chords. At the far corner Nora Bluntik, my former Department Head, stood looking like a copy of Edvard Munk's picture; the black hole of her mouth, wide open in the middle of her deadly white face, emitted no sound. Instead, the ghastly whining voice of some pop group's star kept on

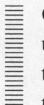

Clouds of blood unravelling under the water made the fish retreat

repeating a chorus line of some samba or cha-cha-cha, as if asking me through the loudspeakers, How Can I Sleep With Your Voice in My Head? Then, suddenly, the music was switched off.

In the total silence that followed, I crossed the expanse of the synthetic red carpet and approached the bar. I asked the barman to call the police. "I want to report the murder that I've just committed," I said. My voice—that legendary velvety baritone—restored miraculously to its full glory, sounded, as in the golden years of the Cold War, rich in undertones, with impeccable rhythmic cadences and clear articulation of every syllable, as required in a good stage delivery, when your well-trained diaphragm makes your voice box free of any constraints. ✖

Zinovy Zinik is a Moscow-born author who has been living in London since 1976. He has published 14 books of prose including novels, short story collections and essays. His short stories and his novel Russian Service were adapted for Radio 3 and his novel The Mushroom Picker was made into a film by the BBC (1993). Zinik's shorter prose appear in The New Yorker, The Spectator, The Guardian amongst others

51(04):78/91|DOI:10.1177/03064220221144918

The unbeaten

Acclaimed writer **ANDREY KURKOV** sits down with **JEMIMAH STEINFELD** to discuss a lifetime of writing against Soviet and Russian oppression

UKRAINE'S MOST CELEBRATED writer Andrey Kurkov is known for his sense of humour, but since Russia's invasion of Ukraine earlier this year he said he's almost lost it. It's been rekindled courtesy of new jokes that have emerged in the country, ones that poke fun at Russians and display Ukrainian resilience.

"It's very good, I'm very happy about this development," Kurkov tells me over coffee. Obviously I'm keen to hear one and he's more than happy to oblige.

"A Ukrainian is asked 'Are you ready for the nuclear end of the world?' and the Ukrainian responds 'Yes, I am ready and I have plans for six months afterwards'." He lets out a wry chuckle.

We're sitting in a crowded café in central London. It's a privilege to be with him, not just because he's the titan of Ukrainian literature (and he really is – his work is the most translated into English of any living Ukrainian writer, alongside some 30 other languages). Also because of how in demand he is. Since 24 February, Kurkov has become the go-to for editors seeking analysis on the country. For a man who has stayed put in Ukraine even though he was displaced from his home in Kyiv earlier in the war, he writes and speaks with impressive regularity. All the while his Twitter feed provides one of the most insightful records of the war, a sombre chronicle of life under Russian bombardment with a light-hearted garnish (on 8 November, for example, he tweeted about the opening of a new

McDonalds in a village outside of Kyiv that is the first to come with its own bomb shelter. "Stay safe and order cheese-burger!" he wrote).

When we meet, at 10am, he's already been on Sky News and will soon head off on a book-signing tour at a dozen bookshops across London. None of these are even the day's main event. He's in London to attend the Index on Censorship Freedom of Expression Awards in the evening, at which he is very much the man of the hour – the winner of the Trustees Award for his contributions to free expression. It's a richly deserved award and one that feels very personal to Index; we were the first to publish Kurkov in translation, back in the early 1990s, a fact he will not forget himself.

Kurkov's experiences of and contributions to free expression are vast. Born in 1961 in the Leningrad region before moving to live with his grandmother in Kyiv (she was a doctor and lived in the grounds of a children's tuberculosis sanitorium), Kurkov remembers lots of children's books about Lenin, "ideologically correct ones", and chose to read medical books on surgery instead because they were "better quality; the illustrated ones were much more bright and horrible."

While Kurkov's earliest experiences →

LEFT. Andrey Kurkov in Sofiiska Square, Kyiv on 15 November 2021 during the Vacant Chairs rally held in support of Ukrainian political prisoners illegally imprisoned in Russia and its occupied regions

He wrote children's stories by way of mental escape from prison

RIGHT: Kurkov at a checkpoint as he went west from his home in Kyiv

→ of writing date to childhood (aged seven he penned a poem imagining the life of his deceased hamster), his first formal foray into writing was when he was a prison guard in Odessa in the 1980s. There he wrote children's stories by way of "mental escape from prison".

His sharp, acerbic prose didn't fit the Soviet agenda and Kurkov's own story quickly morphed into the classic author tale of rejection after rejection, with a Communist twist.

"I got rejection letters from everyone. And then I gave The Favourite Son of Cosmopolitan to the head editor of a publishing house and two weeks later he said that it's a brilliant novel but it will be never published because it's not Soviet literature."

He did though find "illegal success" through the *samizdat* network. His texts were circulated widely – as far as Vladivostok on Russia's far eastern coast – and he'd tour the Soviet Union, doing readings in underground venues. In one instance he read a book of his in a single four-hour sitting. None of this was ideal of course, but to my sheltered ears it has an air of romance.

"It was romantic," he said in agreement. "It was a very exciting time. I was invited because of my manuscripts to come to Riga in the Baltic States and I was staying in the houses of people I'd never met," he added.

Was it dangerous, I ask? Kurkov shakes his head.

His first $100 from publishing was used to purchase a bulletproof door for his home

"My brother was a dissident. He was arrested and given a suspended sentence and given the diagnosis of schizophrenia as a punishment. His friends were arrested and some of them died in detention, but among my friends we never had problems. We knew we were followed and some were reported but nothing happened. Because it was fiction, satirical stuff."

The idea that fiction offered writers a level of protection comes up again when Kurkov tells me about the years immediately following the Soviet Union collapse, when Ukraine became "a criminal state". Kurkov found himself flogging his books on a busy street in Kyiv. There he was approached by a man from a protection racket who offered to protect him for free.

"The mafia had respect always for artists and writers," he said.

Of course fiction could only offer a level of protection and Kurkov was not immune to the struggles Ukraine was facing. His first $100 he made from publishing a book was used to purchase a bullet-proof door for his home, for example (Soviet doors were no use, made "almost of paper"). Kurkov also had to deal with the very tangible problems of there being no publishing houses in Ukraine and, worse still, no paper. This paved the way for one of his wilder tales, in which he borrowed $16,000 and bought six tonnes of paper from Kazakhstan, which he used to print 75,000 copies of two of his books (Bickford's Fuse, and the children's book Adventures of baby-vacuum-cleaner Gosha). A gruelling process, the printers were apparently drunk all summer. He

CREDIT: Andrey Kurkov

then stored the books in his apartment in tunnels that looped from sofa to toilet to kitchen, all the while heading to busy streets in Kyiv to sell them.

"I made myself cardboard with an inscription 'I am the author'," he said. I wish he had a photo (he sadly doesn't).

It took him a year to flog the books and from this he earnt a profit of $700, which he duly spent on his first computer.

Kurkov writes mostly in Russian and is fluent in many languages including, somewhat surprisingly, Japanese. He could have gone down many different, less difficult paths. But he tells me he knew he always wanted to be a fiction writer. His life did become easier when his novel, Death and the Penguin, was published in 1996. It went on to become a bestseller and was translated into English in 2001. And while Ukraine's history continued to take twists and turns, the drama provided a good stage for his work. His 2018 book Grey Bees, for example, imagines the conflict raging in his country through the adventures of a mild-mannered beekeeper.

But when Russia invaded Ukraine earlier this year it was one step too far for his creative spirit. Kurkov was in the process of writing a new novel, which was immediately aborted and hasn't been picked up since. The escapist impulse that drove his first book is impossible to muster today, he tells me. So he concentrates on non-fiction instead.

"I write every day about what is happening in Ukraine. Every morning I get in touch with my friends in Ukraine in different places. I am in touch with people who are under occupation. I am following what is happening and I am writing about the issues which I consider the most important – not about battles because I am not an expert – but about the life of civilians. This is the only thing I can do professionally," he said.

Kurkov does not appear unhappy to be a spokesperson for the nuances of his country. Indeed he almost looks offended when I ask him if it's a heavy burden and directs the conversation

towards how the war has changed the Ukraine language. Military jargon has infiltrated conversations about Russia, while a rise in hate speech has made vocabulary more charged.

"There is an attempt to force everyone to agree with the same formulas and same narratives in counter propaganda," he said, listing calls to cancel Russian culture as one example.

"This is a very hot issue and it creates immediately very heated discussions. And the issue of not taking part in events with Russians, even if they're against Putin, and we're all against Putin." He mentions a meeting with Mikhail Shishkin, the bestselling Russian novelist, and the hundreds of attacks that ensued. Kurkov was called a collaborator, a traitor and a Russian agent.

It seems farcical that such labels would be used against Kurkov. He's president of PEN Ukraine and has spent his life promoting Ukraine literature and culture abroad. Fortunately the name slinging hasn't stopped his commitment to Ukrainian culture. Writing in Index earlier this year, Kurkov outlined the various ways it had been attacked in the 20th century and how "today's Ukrainian intellectuals face the same danger". Russian bombs were raining down on museums; libraries were being destroyed and ransacked, shelves cleared of books written in Ukrainian; intellectuals were being arrested and killed. Months on from this article, and despite the turning tide on the battlefield, Kurkov says the situation has not improved. The work to protect Ukraine's culture remains as urgent. Just days before we meet, Kurkov says they've received news that the body of Volodymyr Vakulenko, a children's book author who was kidnapped back in March, had been located.

"We found mention of his name in the book of a local mortuary, which said that he was buried in grave number 319, so a couple of days ago this grave was opened," he said. A body was found

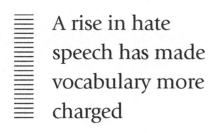

A rise in hate speech has made vocabulary more charged

there, though it later turned out to not be his. The search continues.

Before he was kidnapped, Vakulenko had hidden a hand-written diary in his garden under an apple tree, which has been found. It will, pending permission from the author's son, be published and Kurkov wants people to read it.

He also wants people to learn about Crimean Tartars, a Sunni Muslim indigenous ethnic group whose roots in the region go back to at least the 13th century. They've been a particular target of Russia since the annexation of Crimea in 2014 and yet their story has been forgotten. Kurkov is aware of around 15 Crimean Tartar journalists and activists who are in Russian prisons accused of things that they never did. One of them is minority rights defender and father of four Nariman Dzhelyal, who was sentenced to 17 years in jail this September. He has already been in jail for a year and without international pressure, he will likely be deported to a very remote prison, out of reach from anyone.

All of this is a heavy burden and yet the pretext of our meeting is celebratory – to honour him in person with his Index award. It feels too light on one level, an award during a war. But that doesn't denigrate it.

'It's very important. This is probably the first appreciation I get for what I do," Kurkov said. And with that he is gone, off to his book signings and the many other requests for his thoughts on the war. ✖

Jemimah Steinfeld is editor-in-chief of Index on Censorship

51(04):92/95|DOI:10.1177/03064220221144919

'*Red Memory* left me with not a shred of doubt that the Cultural Revolution is still relevant to understanding modern-day China, as well as the underpinnings of our own twenty-first century cultural clashes.'
Barbara Demick, author of *Nothing to Envy*

'A masterpiece.'
Julia Lovell

'Took my breath away.'
Barbara Demick

'Haunting.'
Oliver Burkeman

RED MEMORY

Living, Remembering and Forgetting
China's Cultural Revolution
TANIA BRANIGAN

ff

An indelible exploration of the Cultural Revolution and how it has shaped China today, *Red Memory* uncovers forty years of silence through the rarely heard stories of individuals who lived through Mao's decade of madness.

faber

Out in hardback, ebook and audiobook February 2023

The smile that says a thousand words

As he prepares to return to the country where he was attacked, Ugandan poet **DANSON KAHYANA** tells **KATIE DANCEY-DOWNS** why his words are suppressed

WHEN DANSON KAHYANA sees a *boda boda*, the motorcycle taxis that zip along busy streets in Kampala, Uganda's capital, he will now always see a potential attack. In April, men riding these vehicles ambushed him, beat him and stole his belongings.

The poet, who is also a Makerere University lecturer and president emeritus of PEN Uganda, spoke to Index on a call from Helsinki, just days before his planned return to Uganda.

As he grinned through the computer screen, his three missing teeth gave a hint at what else he might have lost on that day. "I think I could have lost my life," he said.

While publicly Kahyana referred to what happened as a robbery, he suspects he'd been trailed for a long time.

"I had to decide: do I make this a political thing by accusing the government or do I tone it down and call it a robbery?" he said.

Ultimately, he said he had no hard evidence, and could therefore never make an accusation.

"I didn't want to battle with my wounds and then also battle with legal harassment," Kahyana said, describing how police were likely to call him in repeatedly and ask for evidence if he were to accuse the government

of the attack. Even so, there were specific circumstances that made Kahyana inclined to believe it was not a simple robbery. To begin with, now exiled Ugandan novelist Kakwenza Rukirabashaija said he was tortured by security forces and that his tormentors brought up Kahyana's name.

This fact in isolation was nothing more than gossip, but the robbers also used Kahyana's phone to change his

Gmail password around 12 hours after the attack, and he believes they could have been reading his messages.

His phone remained active until he asked his mobile operator to switch it off, and after paying a private detective for GPS tracking he discovered that the phone was just kilometres from where he lived.

He believes these facts are pointers but, again, are not hard evidence.   →

> You can see that I had to lose my teeth, right?

ABOVE: Poet Danson Kahyana shows the gap where three teeth used to be, lost in a violent attack in his home country of Uganda

Disturbing the peace

Yoweri Museveni has had a grip on Uganda's presidency since 1986, starting his fifth term of office in 2021. That year's elections were marred by widespread violence and the arrests of journalists and opposition supporters. FRANCIS CLARKE looks at the most recent threats to free expression

Ramped-up repression online

The Computer Misuse Act was already seen as repressive, but Museveni signed amendments on six sections into law on 13 October this year that took repression further. One of the aims of the bill is to prohibit the "sending or sharing of misleading, malicious and unsolicited information" online, which has raised concerns that the law could threaten freedom of expression and press freedom in the country. It could also be used to further target critics of the government.

Targeting the press

On 16 March 2022, Norman Tumuhimbise and Bikobere Pharidah, of online broadcaster Alternative Digitalk TV, were charged in a Kampala court with "cyber stalking" Museveni. Their crime was publicising two books by Tumuhimbise – who is both the station's executive director and an author – that shine a light on Museveni's policies from

his nearly four decades of rule. They were accused of "disturbing the peace and quiet of the president of the Republic of Uganda". This did not stop them being signatories to a petition in October challenging the recently-passed Computer Misuse Act amendments.

Criminalisation of LGBTQ+ people

In a country where same-sex sexual activity is illegal, LGBTQ+ people are under constant threat. A May 2021 party held at a Kampala shelter that helps LGBTQ+ youth ended in 44 arrests, with detainees charged with "a negligent act likely to spread infection of disease" as part of the country's harsh penal code. It has since been reported that at least 17 of those arrested were subject to forced anal examinations. The charges were dismissed in court after the prosecution failed to present any witnesses.

Francis Clarke is editorial assistant at Index

→ As we spoke, Kahyana reeled off a list of poetic Facebook posts – each one a potential inciting incident that could have landed him in trouble – along with comment boxes full of thinly veiled death threats.

"Someone tell the life-president to shut up, since there is no more wisdom that comes from his mouth; we are not interested in being demoralised every time he speaks. Let him concentrate on celebrating his major achievement – bringing the country to its knees through a patronage-fuelled grip on

the parliament, the judiciary, the army, the police, and the school system," he wrote in one post. Facebook is banned in Uganda, although the use of VPNs means there is still access.

Kahyana also spent time in the USA as a Fulbright scholar, the geographical distance and experience of a functioning democracy emboldening his criticism of his own country.

After reading out a post critical of the president's wife, Janet Museveni, who was appointed as education and sports minister in 2016, he joked: "You can see

that I had to lose my teeth, right?"

The very day before the attack, Kahyana had written a critical post about the Rwandan president visiting Uganda. Posts like this, Kahyana said, are not completely unusual in Uganda. What is more unusual is that he is a university professor. "The problem is my performance space."

Kahyana arrived in Finland in July after the attack in Kampala. He was signed off work and took the time to rest, while planning to return. The life of an asylum seeker would be very difficult, he said, fearing being left in constant limbo. A few days after speaking to Index, he was set to return to Uganda – keeping his job depends on it and his family is still there.

"When you have a family back home, there's only so much you can say because you're always worried that while you're out of reach for the regime, your family is within reach," he said.

Kahyana recalled the work of Rukirabashaija and poet Stella Nyanzi, who both sought safety in Germany, saying: "If you see what they write and how they write, they write with the space of exile. There are things that they write that you can never write in Uganda."

The *boda boda* attack, whether a vicious robbery or a more sinister attempt at silencing, was not the first time Kahyana had felt threatened. After the palace in Kasese (Kahyana's home district) faced a military assault in 2016 when more than 150 people were killed, Kahyana mobilised Ugandan writers to respond in the book Fire on the Mountain. He said he got a call from someone claiming to be from the government, saying they didn't want the book launched. His uncle received a similar call from the police. While it was not banned outright, the book made it to very few shelves.

In Uganda, he said, the general landscape for free expression is "very bad". He recently presented a document to the Finnish minister of foreign affairs,

If I want to say, 'Fuck you Mr President,' I can't say that

outlining Uganda's criminalisation of peaceful protests, harassment of journalists and the Computer Misuse Act, recently amended so that people can be arrested for "cyber-harassment" or "offensive communication" (see overleaf). Insulting the president online can lead to jail time.

But it is the resulting self-censorship, he believes, which is the most damaging type of censorship.

When Kahyana wrote the poems Lies and On Loss, printed here for the first time, there were considerations he had to make. Even from the safety of Helsinki, the knowledge of his return and his family's safety affected how freely he let his words flow. He carefully picked his language, acknowledging that he is forced to water down what he really wants to say.

"If I want to say, 'Fuck you Mr President,' I can't say that. If I want to say, 'I wish I could grab your balls and wrestle you down,' I can't say that," he told Index.

On Loss begins with the teeth he lost in the attack. "I used to have a beautiful smile. What are the traumas I have? Just look at my teeth. I shudder at what has happened," he said.

Lies comes from a love for his country and a deep sense of betrayal. "[President Yoweri] Museveni came to power in 1986 after a five-year guerrilla struggle. And we all believed that he was a democrat."

After Museveni changed the constitution so that he could continue serving indefinitely, Kahyana felt he had been fed a lie. What he had hoped for was a peaceful handover of power to the next president.

"Even by writing these two poems and wanting to publish them, it's an act of bravery," Kahyana said. "Because the best thing would be to shut up completely." ✖

Katie Dancey-Downs is assistant editor at Index

51(04):97/99|DOI:10.1177/03064220221144920

Lies

They tell us we're free to say whatever we want
For the constitution guarantees the freedom of speech
But when we speak, they declare us enemies of the state
And knock out our teeth to inject fear into our hearts

They tell us we're free to hold peaceful demonstrations
For the constitution guarantees the freedom of assembly
But when we peacefully gather at the freedom square
They unleash the anti-riot brigade upon us and break our skulls.

They tell us we're free to vote for the candidates we desire
For the constitution guarantees us the freedom to choose
But when we vote for the people we love and trust
The rulers terrorise us and scatter us into exile.

They tell us we're the determiners of our destiny
For the constitution bestows power unto us, the citizens,
But when we denounce kleptocracy and tyranny
The armed forces hound us to death, with impunity.

On Loss

I lost three teeth, three lovely teeth
For speaking about my vision of a better-governed country
Where corruption and sectarianism have no place

I lost three teeth, three lovely teeth
For dearly loving this much-abused country
And trying my best to save it from plunderers

I lost three teeth, three lovely teeth
For asking my compatriots to listen to disparate views
Before they consider their own as fool-proof truths.

I lost three teeth, three lovely teeth
For fighting for my basic rights and freedoms
As guaranteed by the constitution of the republic. ✖

Danson Kahyana is a Ugandan writer, associate professor at Makerere University and President Emeritus of PEN Uganda

Truth, down under

Australian poet **DIANE FAHEY** speaks to **FRANCIS CLARKE** about authoritarian manipulation, environmental activism and her new poem, which is printed here

T IS FITTING that on the day Australian poet Diane Fahey spoke to Index about a piece related to authoritarianism, the so-called Trump of the Tropics, Brazilian President Jair Bolsonaro, made his first public remarks following his election defeat to Luiz Inácio Lula da Silva.

"Not for the first time in human history, the Trump era involved very large numbers of people being inveigled by lies. Some simply hoodwinked, some dwelling in a hinterland between truth and lies, and some actively embracing the lie as a substitute for truth," Fahey said.

With former US President Donald Trump out of office and now followed out of the door by Bolsonaro, Fahey discussed her new poem Lemming, which focuses on the collective of people who vote for and support authoritarians. However, she does not necessarily want to apportion blame.

"I want to sharpen my moral focus on the kinds of authoritarian manipulation to which some people are subject, willingly or unconsciously, [and] to hold such authoritarian individuals and systems to account – in the small space of my poem, at least," she said.

The central figure of the poem is, as the title suggests, a lemming. They

TOP: Australian poet Diane Fahey

Lemming

There's no certainty,
even in throwing yourself off a cliff.

You might, after all,
if at the tail-end of the throng

achieve a soft landing
upon a mound of other bodies,

and wake to find yourself
a survivor, damp with sea spray –

a plight soon dealt with,
so Central Command assured us,

by a Guardian ready to euthanise or, in the case of non-lethal injuries,

winch a bandaged subject
up the Great Precipice

to undergo Rehabilitation
before a second attempt:

a Double Honour, in Their eyes: posthumous medals, deep-carved names.

Is that to be my fate?
Right now, I lie in a locked ward,

both legs broken by trampling
just before lift-off,

though the fall itself proved lucky as I landed last, lay nose to the sky.

Let me declare my hand.
I signed on to Rapture.com

to be a secret witness –
a partisan in a cohort of one –

who'd dare to take the dive
so as to write the story.

I went through each step of
the Induction Process:

the Interview (in an empty room, questions emanating from Loudspeakers)

then the Special Summer Camp in an idyllic location

(the Kumbaya of it all,
in the fellowship of fur).
There were discussion groups
on such topics as: "The Fling versus The Dive"

("Fall" out of favour because too passive – besides, it's such a loaded term.)

We sat in a circle in the Lounge.
One participant, a sad visionary,

spoke of hovering, at first,
above the cliff face

then stepping down through air
to stand tall, toes tucked into warm sand.

Another, with a hipster vibe,
thought "do the drop" was a dance move.

Each session ended with a ritual of chanting and champing:

go, go, go! on, on, on!
down, down, down!

There was stringent physical training, too, though with a fun element –

diving boards above vast trampolines. Group runs were scheduled on the hour.

And, always and everywhere,
Speakers on fluted columns whispered,

at high volume: *go, go, go!*
on, on, on! down, down, down!

Finally, Graduation,
the mass swearing of The Oath.

I'll remember always
the Assembly on the Hill, the Starter Gun,

the minute-long marathon
with that last-second stumble

then the whoosh of cold air,   →

are conscious of being a member of a collective, but a quietly and constructively dissenting one. Fahey said she wants people to think of the character as a journalist.

"I think the situation of the lemming in the poem says a lot about the predicament of the journalist today. It's been devastating to see in recent years how much more dangerous that profession has become," she explained.

Also among Fahey's work is a companion piece to Lemming. Focusing on the individual as opposed to the collective, A Liar's Testament explores deception and fraudulence.

"I've taken the very opposite tack from Lemming by plunging myself into the arch-liar's mind – I was interested in the psychology of lying but also, of course, its contemporary political relevance," Fahey said.

"The possibilities for deception and fraudulence, by individuals and by actors operating on a mass scale, seem, now, measureless. It is frightening, and I struggle to keep up. But it is important to do just that, and to take the measure as one can."

Fahey's poetry features both distinctively Australian and European themes and settings, with a strong focus on Ireland. Her Irish ancestry has left her with a deep identification with its people and culture.

"The particular kinds of political oppression that have been experienced by the Irish people cut deep with me. The tragedies and sorrows of the past remain a powerful presence in Ireland," she said.

"Perhaps the greatest insult done to any people subject to imperial incursions is not the theft of measureless resources, or the violent dispossessions and conflicts, but the attempt to diminish the humanity of those subject to those thefts and that overt physical violence."

In Fahey's home country, her greatest concern around freedom of speech involves the whole Australian community listening to the voices of the First Nations.

"I hope the already strong   →

→ fear and freedom colliding.

Below me, squeals of ecstasy
gave way to hushed awe

as down I sped in the wake of
the great blind shadow.

The cleansed beach waiting.
Each landing a muffled plop

Needless to say, I survived the drop, injured but salvageable,
was repatriated for Treatment:
to live to fall another day.

In the Reclamation Unit –
wire mesh on windows, no paper or pens –

the chart at the end of my bed
has a sketch of two legs, crossed-out,

and is stamp-marked "Gonzo Alert". Somehow, They Know.

So, no scoop, an irksome disability and, increasingly likely, no future.

They've scheduled the second drop for next Thursday,

want me in the vanguard this time – but, with no chance of my joining in the Run,

I'll be taken to the brink by Ambulance, pushed off by the exultant horde.

In this terminal twilight
I find myself imagining

the submerged continent of Lemuria where, it has been said,

the souls of lemmings go –
perhaps living ones, too,

who become, somehow,
amphibian, find a way.

I lie here, raised legs in plaster,
tethered to metal,

writing the Big Exposé in my head and watching a swaying light bulb

cast shadow waves on the ceiling – oceanic, mesmeric.

→ support for the referendum on Voice, Treaty, Truth will grow to the point of producing a resounding 'Yes'," she said.

The referendum, promised by the new Labor government, refers to the Uluru Statement from the Heart, which calls for changes in the constitution and a First Nations voice to parliament, so Indigenous people can be involved in the policies which impact their communities. They also ask for "a process of agreement-making and truth-telling about our history".

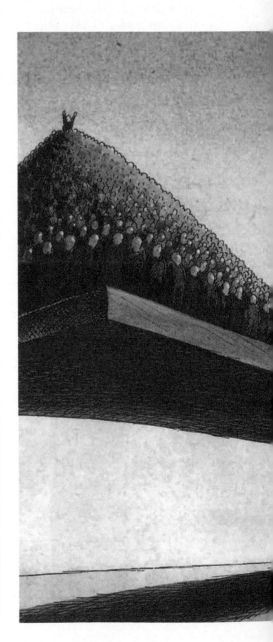

Beyond authoritarianism, a dominant theme of Fahey's work is the planet.

"In the natural world, most change and growth does indeed begin slowly, but can become exponentially rapid and diverse. In the human world, in the human psyche, there can be great resistance to change, even when there is evidence of dangerous threats, as from the climate crisis now," she said.

She believes that the main thrust of resistance should be non-violent protest targeted at the key economic and political players who share responsibility for the continued fossil fuel industry.

"While it is clearly too late for so many human victims and lost creatures and dead forests, it is not too late to put up a fight, a non-violent fight, for so much of the shared life we have on this planet," she said. "In Australian culture and society generally, there are many powerful voices and hands-on activists addressing the problems of climate change, especially as the impacts of natural catastrophes involving fire and extreme flooding have become more devastating – as also, of course, in the global context."

And as a poet, she feels the arts have a key part to play, too, by witnessing the truth, circumventing denial and offering creative problem-solving. Where witnessing truth is concerned, this is perhaps not so different from the aims of Lemming.

Francis Clarke is editorial assistant at Index on Censorship and the current Tim Hetherington fellow

I've started to dream of
a mega-breaker that – surprise! surprise! –

would rush in at the critical moment then carry me out –

far out, away, away –
to Lemuria.

Only that could save me now –
or some red-berried thorn bush

protruding like a hook
below the lip of the cliff.
Desperate times, desperate fantasies…
Perhaps, on Thursday,

I'll tip myself over, go on my own terms.
At least I will be alone,

beautifully alone, as I plummet –
upright, the ocean filling my eyes.

That would make, if ever told,
a good story.

The myth of lemmings killing themselves by jumping off cliffs dates from the 19th century. In an 1877 issue of Popular Science Monthly, apparently suicidal lemmings are presumed to be swimming the Atlantic Ocean in search of the submerged continent of Lemuria. ✖

Diane Fahey is an award-winning Australian poet

51(04):100/103|DOI:10.1177/03064220221144921

LAST WORD

Hair apparent

An interview with **Masih Alinejad**, an Iranian journalist and activist, on the current protests and her hopes for the end of the Islamic Republic

MASIH ALINEJAD WAS born in the small village of Qomi Kola in northern Iran. She became politically active at a young age and was arrested at the age of 18 for producing leaflets critical of the government. In 2014, she launched My Stealthy Freedom, where she invited Iranian women to post pictures of themselves without a hijab. Three years later, she wrote a book about her experiences in the country. The publication of Wind in My Hair: My Fight for Freedom in Modern Iran led journalist Tina Brown to call Alinejad "a flame-thrower for the rights of all women who live under the thumb of repression and injustice".

Since 2019, anyone sending Alinejad videos has been threatened with 10 years in prison. However, since the death in custody of Mahsa Amini in September 2022, her social media accounts have been filled with hard-hitting testimony from protesters around the country.

INDEX How did you become an activist?

MASIH ALINEJAD I became an activist in high school. I just wanted what all teenagers wanted - more freedom. At high school we formed a club and read books on history and politics that we could find and published a newsletter, which was forbidden. There was nothing controversial but we talked about liberty and democracy, which I guess was a bad move. Very soon, all of us were arrested and I spent some time in jail and received a suspended sentence, which meant I couldn't attend university.

Later I became a journalist and decided that I wanted to focus on areas that were neglected by policymakers and other journalists. I investigated corruption and mismanagement and that landed me in trouble again and again.

In 2009, around the time of the Green Protests, I was forced to leave the country or be jailed. In exile, as a journalist I focused on human rights violations of the Islamic Republic and became a voice for the victims of the regime. In 2014, I launched My Stealthy Freedom campaign against compulsory hijab laws in Iran.

INDEX What is the #WhiteWednesdays campaign?

MASIH ALINEJAD The White Wednesday campaign started in May 2017, as an initiative of My Stealthy Freedom, and it was about taking our campaign from social media into the streets of Iran. MSF had started as a Facebook campaign and we were bombarded with videos and pictures from women inside Iran sending pictures and videos of themselves without hijab. After three years, it seemed the time had come to challenge the authorities. Women would go without hijab or wear white on Wednesdays to show their opposition to the compulsory hijab rules.

INDEX How much are Iranians aware of the deaths of young people, particularly women and girls, in the recent protests?

MASIH ALINEJAD The whole of Iran is aware of the deaths and the revolution that is under way. More than 400 people have been killed and at least another 15,000 have been arrested. The regime is threatening more crackdowns.

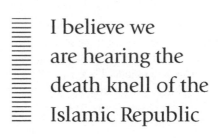

I believe we are hearing the death knell of the Islamic Republic

INDEX Do the internet shutdowns have a large impact on the ability of people to hear the news?

MASIH ALINEJAD When the world is not watching, the regime goes on a murdering rampage. We have seen internet shutdowns in the Kurdish region, in the Baluch region and in parts of the country that faced heavy crackdowns. That's why it's important for democratic countries to provide access to the internet to the Iranian people.

INDEX Have the protests achieved an unstoppable momentum?

MASIH ALINEJAD I believe we are hearing the death knell of the Islamic Republic. It is the beginning of the end. But it's also important to remember that we are in a marathon and not in a 100-metre race.

INDEX If you were detained and could take one book to jail with you, what would it be?

MASIH ALINEJAD The Wind in My Hair, so that my jailers could read it.

INDEX What piece of art has moved you the most?

MASIH ALINEJAD I am moved by human interactions.

INDEX What news headline would you most like to read?

MASIH ALINEJAD Islamic Republic consigned to the dustbin of history. ✖

51(04):104/104|DOI:10.1177/03064220221144922